Introduction to Property and Casualty Insurance

Introduction to Property and Casualty Insurance

First Edition • Second Printing

American Institute for Chartered Property Casualty
Underwriters/Insurance Institute of America
720 Providence Road, Suite 100
Malvern, Pennsylvania 19355-3433

© 2008
American Institute for Chartered Property Casualty Underwriters/Insurance Institute of America

All rights reserved. This book or any part thereof may not be reproduced without the written permission of the copyright holder.

Unless otherwise apparent, examples used in AICPCU/IIA materials related to this course are based on hypothetical situations and are for educational purposes only. The characters, persons, products, services, and organizations described in these examples are fictional. Any similarity or resemblance to any other character, person, product, services, or organization is merely coincidental. AICPCU/IIA is not responsible for such coincidental or accidental resemblances.

This material may contain Internet Web site links external to AICPCU/IIA. AICPCU/IIA neither approves nor endorses any information, products, or services to which any external Web sites refer. Nor does AICPCU/IIA control these Web sites' content or the procedures for Web site content development.

AICPCU/IIA specifically disclaims any implied warranties of merchantability or fitness for a particular purpose. No warranty may be created or extended by sales representatives or written sales materials.

AICPCU/IIA materials related to this course are provided with the understanding that AICPCU/IIA is not engaged in rendering legal, accounting, or other professional service. Nor is AICPCU/IIA explicitly or implicitly stating that any of the processes, procedures, or policies described in the materials are the only appropriate ones to use. The advice and strategies contained herein may not be suitable for every situation.

Information which is copyrighted by and proprietary to Insurance Services Office, Inc. ("ISO Material") is included in this publication. Use of the ISO Material is limited to ISO Participating Insurers and their Authorized Representatives. Use by ISO Participating Insurers is limited to use in those jurisdictions for which the insurer has an appropriate participation with ISO. Use of the ISO Material by Authorized Representatives is limited to use solely on behalf of one or more ISO Participating Insurers.

This publication includes forms which are provided for review purposes only. These forms may not be used, in whole or in part, by any company or individuals not licensed by Insurance Services Office, Inc. (ISO) for the applicable line of insurance and jurisdiction to which this form applies. It is a copyright infringement to include any part(s) of this form within independent company programs without the written permission of ISO.

First Edition • Second Printing • September 2009

Library of Congress Control Number: 2008930702

ISBN 978-0-89463-363-8

Foreword

The American Institute for Chartered Property Casualty Underwriters and the Insurance Institute of America (the Institutes) are not-for-profit organizations committed to meeting the evolving educational needs of the risk management and insurance community. The Institutes strive to provide current, relevant educational programs in formats that meet the needs of risk management and insurance professionals and the organizations that employ them.

The American Institute for CPCU (AICPCU) was founded in 1942 through a collaborative effort between industry professionals and academics, led by faculty members at The Wharton School of the University of Pennsylvania. In 1953, AICPCU coordinated operations with the Insurance Institute of America (IIA), which was founded in 1909 and remains the oldest continuously functioning national organization offering educational programs for the property-casualty insurance sector.

The Insurance Research Council (IRC), founded in 1977, is a division of AICPCU supported by industry members. This not-for-profit research organization examines public policy issues of interest to property-casualty insurers, insurance customers, and the general public. IRC research reports are distributed widely to insurance-related organizations, public policy authorities, and the media.

The Institutes' customer- and solution-focused business model allows us to better serve the risk management and insurance communities. Customer-centricity defines our business philosophy and shapes our priorities. The Institutes' innovation arises from our commitment to finding solutions that meet customer needs and deliver results. Our business process is shaped by our commitment to efficiency, strategy, and responsible asset management.

The Institutes believe that professionalism is grounded in education, experience, and ethical behavior. The Chartered Property Casualty Underwriter (CPCU) professional designation offered by the Institutes is designed to provide a broad understanding of the property-casualty insurance industry. Depending on professional needs, CPCU students may select either a commercial or a personal risk management and insurance focus. The CPCU designation is conferred annually by the AICPCU Board of Trustees.

In addition, the Institutes offer designations and certificate programs in a variety of disciplines, including the following:

- Claims
- Commercial underwriting
- Fidelity and surety bonding
- General insurance
- Insurance accounting and finance
- Insurance information technology
- Insurance production and agency management
- Insurance regulation and compliance
- Management
- Marine insurance
- Personal insurance
- Premium auditing
- Quality insurance services
- Reinsurance
- Risk management
- Surplus lines

You can complete a program leading to a designation, take a single course to fill a knowledge gap, or take multiple courses and programs throughout your career. The practical and technical knowledge gained from Institute courses enhances your qualifications and contributes to your professional growth. Most Institute courses carry college credit recommendations from the American Council on Education. A variety of courses qualify for credits toward certain associate, bachelor's, and master's degrees at several prestigious colleges and universities.

Our Knowledge Resources Department, in conjunction with industry experts and members of the academic community, develops our trusted course and program content, including Institute study materials. These materials provide practical career and performance-enhancing knowledge and skills.

We welcome comments from our students and course leaders. Your feedback helps us continue to improve the quality of our study materials.

Peter L. Miller, CPCU
President and CEO
American Institute for CPCU
Insurance Institute of America

Preface

Introduction to Property and Casualty Insurance is the text for the INTRO course. This course is designed to provide an overview of property and casualty insurance at a basic level. It is recommended as a starting point for those who are new to insurance or the property and casualty insurance field or who are starting their insurance education.

The ten chapters of this text can be summarized as follows:

- Chapter 1 discusses basic insurance concepts, including risk, transfer, and pooling.
- Chapter 2 provides an overview of the insurance transaction and identifies the parties to the transaction.
- Chapter 3 discusses how insurers are categorized and the functions that they perform.
- Chapter 4 discusses the purpose of underwriting, the major activities in the underwriting process, and how an insurer's underwriting results are measured.
- Chapter 5 describes the claim function and the activities in the claim handling process.
- Chapter 6 discusses the structure of insurance policies and identifies common insurance policy provisions.
- Chapter 7 identifies the common personal property and liability loss exposures and the coverages available to protect against them.
- Chapter 8 discusses the common commercial property loss exposures and the coverages available to protect against them.
- Chapter 9 identifies the common commercial liability loss exposures and the coverages available to protect against them.
- Chapter 10 discusses how insurance premiums are determined and how insurance rates are developed.

The Institutes extend sincere thanks to those insurance professionals, course leaders, and sponsors who provided guidance during the planning of this text and particularly to Roy Brandow and Terry Macko, who reviewed the manuscript. Their thoughtful review of the material helped to ensure that the text is accurate and reflects current industry practice.

For more information about the Institutes' programs, please call our Customer Service Department at (800) 644-2101, e-mail us at customerservice@cpcuiia.org, or visit our Web site at www.aicpcu.org.

American Institute for CPCU
Insurance Institute of America

Contributors

The American Institute for CPCU and the Insurance Institute of America acknowledge with deep appreciation the contributions made to the content of this text by the following persons:

Arthur L. Flitner, CPCU, ARM, AIC
AICPCU/IIA

Susan Kearney, CPCU, ARM, AAI
AICPCU/IIA

Charles Nyce, PhD, CPCU, ARM
AICPCU/IIA

Donna J. Popow, JD, CPCU, AIC
AICPCU/IIA

Rich Berthelsen, JD, CPCU, ARM
AICPCU/IIA

Pamela J. Brooks, CPCU, AIM, AAM
AICPCU/IIA

Mary Ann Cook, CPCU, AU, AAI
AICPCU/IIA

Martin J. Frappolli, CPCU, FIDM, AIS
AICPCU/IIA

Ann E. Myhr, CPCU, ASLI, ARM
AICPCU/IIA

Karen K. Porter, JD, CPCU, ARP, AIS
AICPCU/IIA

Lowell S. Young, CPCU, CLU, APA
AICPCU/IIA

Contents

Chapter 1
Insurance Overview	1.1
Basic Insurance Concepts	1.3
The Law of Large Numbers	1.5
Types of Insurance Policies	1.7
How Insurance Benefits Society	1.10
Premium Allocation	1.14
Summary	1.15

Chapter 2
Insurance Marketing	2.1
The Insurance Transaction	2.3
Producer Functions	2.5
Insurance Marketing Systems	2.8
Summary	2.10

Chapter 3
Insurance Services	3.1
Classifications and Types of Insurers	3.3
Insurer Functions	3.10
Insurance Regulation	3.14
Summary	3.21

Chapter 4
Underwriting Basics	4.1
Purpose of Underwriting	4.3
The Underwriting Process	4.4
Measuring Underwriting Results	4.9
Summary	4.13

Chapter 5
Claims Basics	5.1
Goals of the Claim Function	5.3
Activities in the Claim Handling Process	5.5
Roles of Claim Personnel	5.10
Measuring Claim Results	5.16
Summary	5.19

Chapter 6
Insurance Coverage	6.1
Physical Structure of Insurance Policies	6.3
Common Policy Provisions	6.7
Policy Analysis	6.13
Summary	6.15

Chapter 7
Personal Insurance	7.1
Personal Property and Liability Loss Exposures	7.3
Homeowners Insurance Policy	7.4
Personal Auto Insurance Policy	7.7
Other Personal Insurance Policies	7.12
Summary	7.16

Chapter 8
Commercial Property Insurance	8.1
Commercial Property Loss Exposures	8.3
Commercial Property Insurance Coverage	8.7
Summary	8.14

Chapter 9
Commercial Liability Insurance	9.1
Commercial Liability Loss Exposures	9.3
Commercial Liability Insurance Coverages	9.7
Summary	9.11

Chapter 10
Premium Determination	10.1
How an Insurance Premium Is Determined	10.3
Developing Insurance Rates	10.6
Types of Rates and Rating Basis	10.11
Types of Rating Plans	10.19
Summary	10.22

Index	1

Direct Your Learning

Insurance Overview

Educational Objectives

After learning the content of this chapter and completing the corresponding course guide assignment, you should be able to:

- Explain why the concepts of risk, transfer, and pooling are essential to insurance.
- Explain how the law of large numbers applies to insurance.
- Identify the common types of personal and commercial insurance policies available to cover customers' needs.
- Explain how insurance benefits society.
- List the ways in which insurers allocate the premiums they collect.

Outline

Basic Insurance Concepts

The Law of Large Numbers

Types of Insurance Policies

How Insurance Benefits Society

Premium Allocation

Summary

Insurance Overview

BASIC INSURANCE CONCEPTS

The concepts of risk, transfer, and pooling are important components of the insurance mechanism.

Many businesses and families have concerns about the possible financial impact of an unforeseen event, such as a fire or an auto accident. An insurance policy can help to alleviate some of these concerns by providing a source of payment for the costs of such events.

Insurance is a mechanism by which risk is transferred by a person or business to an **insurer**, which reimburses the insured for covered losses and provides for the sharing of losses among all insureds. This sharing is possible because the insurer collects a pool of all of the **premiums** paid by customers into a fund from which it pays losses. The insurance mechanism, therefore, includes three essential components:

- Risk
- Transfer
- Pooling

Risk

The first component of the insurance mechanism is **risk**. This idea of risk is a fundamental insurance concept. Individuals and families face uncertainty from the possible financial consequences of **loss exposures** such as fire, weather-related or other damage to their homes, and lawsuits or injuries arising from an auto accident. Business owners are concerned about the financial consequences of injuries to customers while on the business premises or to employees in the course of their jobs. They are also concerned about potential costs arising from physical damage to owned buildings or personal property, loss of profit from an interruption of their business, burglary or robbery, and many other possible loss exposures.

Transfer

The second component of the insurance mechanism is **transfer**. The financial consequences of unanticipated events can be transferred to an insurer, thus reducing the risk or uncertainty associated with these costs. Losses may still occur, but the insured's uncertainty regarding their financial impact is reduced because a mechanism for paying the costs of these losses has been put in

---

Insurance
A risk management technique that transfers the potential financial consequences of certain specified loss exposures from the insured to the insurer.

Insurer
A company that sells insurance policies to protect insureds against financial hardship caused by financial losses.

Premium
The price of the insurance coverage provided for a specified period.

Risk
The uncertainty about outcomes, some of which can be negative.

Loss exposure
Any condition or situation that presents a possibility of loss, regardless of whether loss actually occurs.

Transfer
In the context of risk management, a risk financing technique by which the financial responsibility for losses and variability in cash flows is shifted to another party.

Insurance policy
A contract that states the agreement between and the rights and duties of the insurer and insured.

place. For example, when an individual purchases a new home, he or she will purchase an **insurance policy** to reduce the financial uncertainties related to the ownership of that home and to provide for the payment of losses that may occur. When insureds transfer their risks of financial loss to an insurer, they are exchanging the possibility of large, uncertain loss amounts for smaller, more certain premium amounts. Risks are transferred to an insurer through the use of an insurance policy.

Risk is not always transferred to an insurer; in some circumstances, the risk or uncertainty regarding losses can be contractually transferred to a third party. Such a transfer occurs when a general contractor requires subcontractors to carry insurance to protect the general contractor. Rather than transferring the financial consequences of losses to an insurer, the general contractor transfers them to a subcontractor. Most likely, the subcontractor would then transfer the financial consequences it has assumed to an insurer by purchasing an insurance policy that includes coverage for the general contractor. The subcontractor is willing to assume these financial consequences because doing so allows it to earn additional income by performing work for the general contractor. Likewise, the landlord for a large commercial structure might hold its tenants responsible for damage to the premises as part of the lease or rental agreement. From the landlord's perspective, the uncertainty about paying losses arising from the ownership of the building has been transferred to the tenants. The chance of loss has not been reduced or eliminated, but the financial consequences of losses that do occur have been shifted from the landlord to the tenant. The tenants are willing to accept the potential consequences in order to comply with the lease requirements and to occupy the premises. Therefore, each party to the lease agreement gains some benefit from the transaction.

Pooling

Pooling
An arrangement that facilitates the grouping together of loss exposures and the resources to pay for any losses that may occur.

The third component of the insurance mechanism is **pooling**. Insurers combine all of the premiums collected from customers into a fund that is used to pay losses as they occur. This means that all insureds share the costs of one another's losses. In effect, the cost of paying for losses that occur for relatively few insureds is spread among all members of the group. This method of sharing of costs among all insureds makes each individual's premium relatively small. For example, the premium to insure a family home valued at $250,000 may be only $2,000 per year, even though the policy may pay the entire $250,000 in the event the house were to be totally destroyed by a covered peril, such as fire.

> ### Risk, Transfer, and Pooling: An Example
>
> Frank has just purchased a new car and is concerned that an auto accident could cause him a large financial loss (risk). Frank pays Insurer A $2,000 to insure his car for one year (transfer). Fortunately, Frank has no accidents during the year. Karla pays Insurer A $2,500 to insure her car for one year. Unfortunately, during a rainstorm that year, Karla's car skids into another car, and Karla is injured. Karla's auto insurance pays $7,450 to repair her car, $8,300 to repair the other car, and $9,000 for Karla's medical bills.
>
> Karla's insurer can pay this loss because it has collected adequate premiums from Frank and many other insureds who did not have losses (pooling). Frank, Karla, and all of the other insureds were willing to pay a premium to transfer their risk to the insurer. In effect, all of the premiums went into a pool from which Karla's loss was paid. In other words, Frank and others shared the cost of Karla's loss.

THE LAW OF LARGE NUMBERS

The law of large numbers assists insurers in making reliable estimates of future loss amounts.

Insurers collect premiums from many insureds and then pool those premiums to pay losses to a relative few insureds. Because all insureds pay premiums but not all suffer losses, the total costs of losses that do occur are spread among all insureds. Insurers determine the premium that each insured will pay by estimating anticipated future loss amounts. These estimates of future loss amounts are based on the amounts paid for actual losses in the past.

The **law of large numbers** is a mathematical principle stating that as the number of homogeneous, independent **exposure units** in a group increases, the relative accuracy of predictions about future outcomes of the group (such as losses to that same group) also increases. This means that, as the number of homeowners policies an insurer issues increases, the accuracy of its predictions about the future losses of the group to whom it has sold homeowners policies also will increase. Conversely, if a group contains only a small number of independent exposure units, its future outcomes cannot be accurately predicted.

For example, assume that the chance of any one homeowner experiencing a loss (frequency of loss) is 1 percent (or 1 in 100). Further assume Insurer A sells one homeowners insurance policy in each of ten different cities, for a total of ten policies. If none of the ten policyholders experiences a loss, the group has no losses (a 0 percent frequency of loss). If one policyholder experiences a loss, the group's actual loss frequency is 10 percent (1 in 10). Similarly, if two policyholders suffer losses, the group's actual loss frequency is 20 percent (2 in 10). The group's performance, (0 percent, 10 percent, and 20 percent) differs significantly from the expected loss frequency of 1 percent for homeowners insurance.

Law of large numbers
A mathematical principle stating that as the number of similar but independent exposure units increases, the relative accuracy of predictions about future outcomes (losses) also increases.

Exposure unit
A fundamental measure of the loss exposure assumed by an insurer.

As Insurer A sells more homeowners policies, the size of the group of insureds will increase. As the group's size increases, Insurer A can anticipate that the performance of the group will get closer and closer to the expected loss frequency of 1 percent because of the operation of the law of large numbers. If Insurer A sells 1,000 policies, this larger group may include five policyholders who suffer losses (.5 percent, or 5 in 1,000), ten who suffer losses (1 percent or 10 in 1,000), or twenty who suffer losses (2 percent, or 20 in 1,000). These performances (.5 percent, 1 percent, and 2 percent) are much closer to the expected loss frequency of 1 percent than the performance of the group that included only ten policyholders. As Insurer A sells more policies, it could expect the group of policyholders' losses to get closer and closer to the expected loss frequency of 1 percent.

> ### Law of Large Numbers—A Noninsurance Example
> One way to consider the operation of the law of large numbers is to examine the results of a series of coin flips. Because there is a 50 percent probability that a flipped coin will land on heads and a 50 percent probability that it will land on tails, a series of coin flips could be expected to yield heads half of the time and tails the other half. However, a coin that is flipped a relatively small number of times (such as 100) may produce a significantly larger number of heads than tails. As the frequency of coin flips increases, the results will get closer and closer to the expected result of 50 percent heads and 50 percent tails.

Although the law of large numbers allows insurers to predict expected loss levels for large groups of policyholders, there is no such method to determine which individual policyholders actually will suffer a loss. For example, if Insurer A sells 1,000 homeowners insurance policies, it can statistically expect ten policyholders from that group to suffer losses (based on the 1 percent expected frequency rate). The law of large numbers does not, however, allow the insurer to predict specifically which policyholders will suffer those losses. It can only indicate that approximately ten policyholders from within that group can be expected to suffer a loss.

The more information an insurer has regarding actual past losses for a particular type of policy (such as for homeowners policies), the more accurately that insurer can forecast the amount of future losses on similar policies. The law of large numbers allows insurers to predict overall losses and then use those predicted loss amounts to determine the individual premiums each insured will pay into the pool of premiums from which future losses will be paid.

For example, as part of calculating rates for automobile coverage, insurers can rely on the law of large numbers to more accurately estimate the number of vehicles that might be stolen or be involved in an accident by reviewing past losses for a large number of similar private passenger exposure units. They can then use those predictions to determine dollar amounts that form the basis of rate calculations for premiums on future auto policies.

In order for the law of large numbers to effectively assist insurers in estimating future losses, there must be not only a large number of exposure units, but the exposure units must be homogeneous and independent. A homogenous group of exposure units means that the characteristics shared by members of the group are similar, but not necessarily identical. For homeowners policies, insurers would group all single-family dwellings of the same construction type separately from two-family dwellings of the same construction type. For automobile policies, insurers would group similar policyholders according to the age and gender of the drivers and the age, type, and use of vehicles.

For exposure units to be independent, the probability of loss to one exposure unit should have no impact on the probability of loss to another exposure unit. For example, the probability that one house in a suburban subdivision will suffer a fire loss is much higher when the house next door already is on fire. Therefore, those two exposure units are not independent. Alternatively, when a vehicle is stolen in Cleveland, Ohio, the theft has no impact on the probability that a vehicle also will be stolen in Portland, Oregon. These two automobile exposure units are, therefore, considered to be independent.

When insurers determine expected loss levels, they exclude catastrophic losses caused by natural events such as earthquakes, hurricanes, or large brush fires, because such events involve many exposure units that are affected by the same cause of loss and that therefore are not considered independent. Insurers estimate potential catastrophe loss amounts using different statistical models because the law of large numbers cannot be used for such losses.

TYPES OF INSURANCE POLICIES

There are many types of personal and commercial insurance policies available to cover the loss exposures of individuals, families, and business organizations.

Insurance producers and insurers can determine their customers' insurance needs based on the customers' personal and commercial loss exposures, which arise out of the ownership of buildings, contents, vehicles, and other property as well as the activities of individuals, families, and business organizations. Once a customer's loss exposures are identified, the policies required to meet that customer's needs may be determined. The types of property-casualty insurance policies available for individuals, families, and business organizations fall into two categories:

- Personal insurance policies
- Commercial insurance policies

Personal Insurance Policies

These are the most common types of personal insurance policies:

- Homeowners
- Personal auto
- Personal watercraft
- Personal umbrella

Personal insurance policies are designed to cover personal loss exposures such as those that arise from buildings, personal property (including contents of the home), physical damage to vehicles, and **legal liability** arising from the ownership of a home, vehicles, or watercraft as well as the activities of individuals and families.

A homeowners policy provides both property and liability coverage. The property coverage protects insureds for damage to the home and its contents caused by fire, wind, lightning, and other causes of loss (**perils**). Most homeowners policies also include coverage for burglary of the contents of the home. Homeowners policies usually exclude or limit coverage for certain classes of valuable property that must instead be covered under a different policy. For example, if an insured owns expensive items of jewelry or an art collection, a personal articles policy or endorsement would be needed to cover the items because the homeowners policy would not provide full coverage for these items. The personal articles policy would cover more perils than the homeowners policy and would include sufficient dollar limits to cover these items. The homeowners policy also includes **personal liability coverage** for legal liability that may arise if someone is injured while on the property (for example, when a visitor falls down the front steps outside of the home or is bitten by the family's pet dog).

A personal auto policy (PAP) covers losses due to bodily injury to another person(s) or damage to property of others arising from an auto accident for which the insured is liable. It also covers damage to the vehicle that results from a **collision** or from fire, theft, wind, contact with a bird or animal, and other causes of loss. A PAP covers only an insured's personal vehicles and excludes commercial vehicles used in connection with a business operation.

The personal liability coverage in the homeowners policy and the auto liability coverage in the PAP exclude or limit coverage for operation of any watercraft. Therefore, an insured who owns a boat may need a separate watercraft policy that covers not only legal liability that may arise from accidents involving the boat but also physical damage to the boat.

An insured that requires higher limits than those available under personal liability or personal auto coverage may also purchase a personal umbrella policy, which provides additional liability limits over those provided by the homeowners, PAP, and watercraft policies. Umbrella policies provide broad coverage and contain relatively few exclusions. Typical limits for a personal umbrella policy are $1 or $2 million or more, which provides an additional level of protection for a very large or unusual type of loss.

Legal liability
The legally enforceable obligation of a person or an organization to pay a sum of money (called damages) to another person or organization.

Peril
The cause of the loss.

Personal liability coverage
Coverage for damages, plus costs of any defense, related to a claim or suit brought against the insured that resulted from bodily injury or property damage caused by an occurrence covered under the policy.

Collision
Damage to a motor vehicle caused by its impact with another vehicle or object, or by the vehicle's overturn.

Commercial Insurance Policies

Personal insurance policies cover only losses that arise from personal loss exposures related to the ownership of a home and personal vehicles. Loss exposures that arise from a business operation are covered under **commercial insurance** policies. These are examples of commercial insurance policies:

- Commercial property
- Commercial crime
- Employee dishonesty
- Commercial general liability
- Commercial auto
- Workers compensation
- Commercial umbrella

A commercial property policy includes coverage for damage to buildings or contents that results from fire, vandalism, and other causes of loss. An insured that occupies but does not own the building does not need to purchase coverage for the building. Such coverage usually is the responsibility of the building's landlord or owner. Many business organizations also need commercial **crime insurance** to protect against theft of contents such as cash registers, computers, inventory, and other business property and of money that could be stolen in a robbery during business hours or in a burglary that occurs after business hours. Crime insurance also can include employee dishonesty coverage for crimes committed by employees (for example, when an employee steals money or inventory from the business).

Commercial general liability (CGL) coverage is also needed to protect the insured against claims that arise from legal liability for bodily injury to others and for damage to the property of others. For example, a retail store could be responsible if a customer falls on the store's wet floor and is injured. Also, if a customer is injured by a product that the business sold, the CGL policy would cover the business owner's legal liability.

Many business organizations purchase a **commercial package policy (CPP)** or a **businessowners policy (BOP)**, policies that combine the needed property, crime, and liability coverages into one policy.

A commercial auto policy protects a business organization against claims for legal liability to others for bodily injury or property damage resulting from the use of vehicles owned or operated by the business. The commercial auto policy also protects against damage to vehicles as the result of collisions and other accidents.

Because employers are required by law to pay certain benefits to employees who are injured on the job or who contract a job-related disease, business organizations also need **workers compensation insurance**, which pays the cost of medical care, lost wages, and other benefits as specified by state law. These benefits are payable regardless of who caused the injury or illness.

Commercial insurance
Insurance that covers for-profit businesses or not-for-profit organizations against the adverse financial effects of property and liability losses.

Crime insurance
Insurance that covers money, securities, merchandise, and other property from various causes of loss such as burglary, robbery, theft, and employee dishonesty.

Commercial general liability (CGL)
Insurance that covers many of the common liability loss exposures faced by an organization, including its premises, operations, and products.

Commercial package policy (CPP)
Policy that covers two or more lines of business by combining ISO's commercial lines coverage parts.

Businessowners policy (BOP)
A package policy that combines most of the property and liability coverages needed by small and medium-sized businesses.

Workers compensation insurance
Insurance that provides coverage for benefits an employer is obligated to pay under workers compensation laws.

Umbrella liability policy
Policy that provides excess coverage over several primary policies (typically CGL, auto, and employers liability) and that may also provide drop-down coverage.

Workers compensation policies do not indicate a limit because the policy will pay the dollar amount required by law. The purchase of an **umbrella liability policy**, which is similar to the personal umbrella policy, is often recommended for business organizations. A commercial umbrella policy provides additional limits beyond those provided by the CGL and commercial auto policies and protects the insured in the event of a large liability loss.

> **Types of Insurance Policies—An Example**
>
> Rob owns a sandwich shop in suburban shopping center. He and his wife, Laurie, also own a two-story single family home approximately five miles from the shop. The home includes an attached garage where Rob and Laurie park their two late-model vehicles, a pickup truck and a minivan. They are concerned that damage to their business or home could result in substantial financial loss. They have contacted their local insurance agent to discuss these concerns and to design an insurance program to meet their personal and commercial needs.
>
> There are many types of property and casualty insurance products available, depending on the needs of the customer. The insurance agent will determine Rob and Laurie's insurance policy needs by examining their loss exposures. Because Rob and Laurie have both personal and commercial loss exposures, they will need both personal and commercial insurance policies.
>
> The personal insurance policies will only cover losses arising out of Rob and Laurie's personal loss exposures related to the ownership of the home and personal vehicles. For loss exposures arising from the sandwich shop operation, Rob will also need commercial insurance policies.

HOW INSURANCE BENEFITS SOCIETY

The insurance industry provides individuals and businesses with many benefits.

The property-casualty insurance industry is a multibillion-dollar industry that not only employs millions of people, but also provides numerous benefits to society. The primary benefit is that, through insurance, individuals and businesses are reimbursed for the costs of covered losses. This loss payment allows individuals and families to recover quickly and businesses to continue operations. A related benefit is that uncertainty about potential future losses is reduced. In addition to loss payment and reducing uncertainty, other benefits of insurance include using resources efficiently, promoting loss control, satisfying legal requirements, and providing a basis for credit.

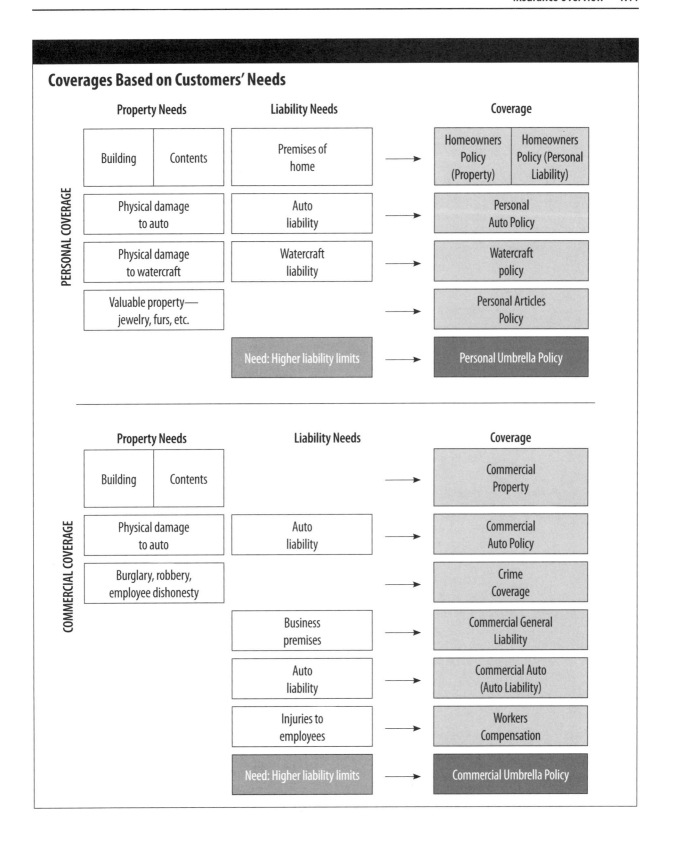

Paying Losses

The major benefit of insurance is indemnifying insureds for covered losses. Through indemnification, individuals and businesses are able to maintain their economic position and avoid becoming a burden on others. For example, when a family's house is destroyed by fire and the loss is covered under an insurance policy, the family will be less dependent on relatives or government organizations for lodging or other continuing expenses. When a business suffers a large loss that is covered under an insurance policy, the business may avoid bankruptcy. Also, the business contributes to society because it can continue to provide jobs for employees, products for its customers, and business for its suppliers. By providing loss payments, insurance contributes to the continued financial strength and stability of individuals, families, and businesses while reducing the uncertainty about future losses.

Reducing Uncertainty

Another benefit of insurance, which is closely related to paying for losses, is the reduction of uncertainty that insurance protection provides. An individual or a family will have increased peace of mind knowing that the possible financial consequences of losses arising from the ownership of a home or a car will be covered by insurance. More entrepreneurs can establish new businesses knowing that the uncertainties related to the financial consequences of some events will be reduced through the purchase of insurance coverage. Existing businesses will be more likely to expand into new operations knowing that insurance coverage is in place for such events. This expansion will benefit society by increasing employment for that business and for businesses in the same community that are providers of services and supplies. When individuals, families, and businesses transfer the uncertainty about the financial consequences of such losses to an insurer, they greatly reduce their financial concerns. Insurers have greater certainty about losses than individuals do, because the law of large numbers enables insurers to predict the number of losses that are likely to occur within the overall pool of insureds and to determine the financial effect of those losses.

Using Resources Efficiently

When individuals and businesses purchase insurance policies, they are, in effect, exchanging small, certain premium amounts for possibly much larger, unknown loss amounts. Insurance makes it unnecessary for individuals and businesses to set aside large amounts of money to pay for the financial consequences of losses that can be insured. Money that would otherwise be set aside to pay for possible losses can be used to improve a family's quality of life or to contribute to the growth of a business. For example, instead of establishing a fund to pay for future losses such as wind damage to buildings or lawsuits resulting from falls on the premises, a business can purchase an insurance policy that will provide a source of payment for such events. When a family purchases a homeowners policy, it avoids the need to set aside a large sum, perhaps $50,000, in savings to be used in the event the house is damaged by fire or other causes of loss. Instead, the family can spend $1,500 for an insurance policy and then use the rest of the $50,000 in savings for another purpose, such as college tuition or retirement savings funds.

Promoting Loss Control

Insurers are interested in lowering the costs of losses and, therefore, promote a variety of loss control activities to their insureds by providing premium reductions for those insureds who practice loss control. These loss control activities can either lower the frequency of potential accidents by preventing losses from happening (loss prevention) or reduce the severity of accidents that occur despite loss prevention activities (loss reduction). For example, individuals and businesses can use fire and burglar alarms to prevent property and crime losses from occurring. Smoke detectors or sprinklers can assist in reducing property losses, and driver training programs can help to reduce the severity of auto losses. Society benefits when losses are controlled because lives are saved and property is preserved. Controlling losses reduces the amount of money insurers must pay out in claims, which allows insurers to reduce insurance costs to all of their customers. Insurers and related organizations employ thousands of safety engineers, loss control representatives, and other specialists to assist in preventing or reducing auto accidents, fires, work-related injuries, injuries caused by defective products, and other types of accidental losses.

Satisfying Legal Requirements

Insurance is often used or required to satisfy legal requirements. In many states, for example, owners of automobiles must prove that they have auto liability insurance before they can register their autos. All states have laws that require employers to pay for job-related injuries or illnesses of their employees, and employers generally purchase workers' compensation insurance to meet this financial obligation.

Providing a Basis for Credit

Insurance is important in the use of credit in our economy. Most banks require property insurance on a home before they will provide a mortgage to help the buyer pay for the home. Banks and leasing companies also require evidence of automobile physical damage insurance before approving an auto loan or a lease agreement for a vehicle. When a business applies for a loan to purchase inventory or production equipment or to lease computer or other office equipment, it might be required to show that the property is insured before the loan or lease is approved.

PREMIUM ALLOCATION

Insurers allocate the premiums they collect to pay losses and to pay expenses. Premium dollars that are not immediately needed for losses or expenses are invested.

Insurers collect millions of dollars of premium each year for the policies they issue to customers. Insurers allocate these premium dollars in three principal ways:

- Pay claims from losses that may happen
- Pay expenses for running the insurance operation
- Invest premium dollars that are not immediately needed

Pay Claims

One way in which insurers allocate collected premiums is claim payment. The primary reason that customers purchase insurance coverage is for payment of covered losses. If a loss occurs, the insured files a claim with the insurer. The insurer's claim department is responsible for investigating the circumstances of the loss and paying the claim. Property insurance claims are generally straightforward and can usually be settled promptly.

Liability insurance claims often involve a lawsuit, trial, and other legal proceedings, which can last for many months or, in some cases, several years. This extended period of time and involvement of attorneys increase the expenses related to settling liability claims. A large portion of the premiums insurers collect are allocated to the payment of losses and the expenses related to claim settlement.

Pay Expenses

A second way in which insurers allocate collected premiums is paying expenses for running the insurance operation. A portion of the collected premiums is used to cover expenses related to selling, issuing, and servicing the policies sold by the insurer. When a policy is sold through an independent agent, the insurer pays commissions to that agent. Also, once the application is submitted to the insurer, many of the insurer's staff are involved in processing the application, issuing a policy, and then providing ongoing customer service once the policy has been issued. The insurer must pay the salaries of underwriters who review applications for acceptability, rating staff who calculate premiums, and processing staff. In addition to paying employee salaries and benefits, insurers also have the same types of operating expenses that any other business would have. These expenses include rent, utilities, taxes, advertising, and similar business-related expenses.

Investments

A third way in which insurers allocate premiums is in investments. An important aspect of the insurance mechanism is that policyholders pay premiums at the start of the policy period, before any losses have happened. Because future loss amounts cannot be predicted with complete accuracy, insurers must build a fund or reserves for the payment of losses in the future. Insurers invest the premium dollars that are not immediately needed to pay losses or expenses.

An insurance operation is considered profitable when the total premiums collected by the insurer are greater than the amounts paid for losses and for all expenses. In those years when the insurance operation earns a profit, any money that remains after losses and expenses have been paid is used to build a fund for contingencies (such as unanticipated catastrophic hurricane or other losses that exceed loss projections) and also to pay dividends to the insurer's stockholders or to policyholders.

In other years, when the insurance operation fails to earn a profit, insurers may use investment income to offset losses that exceed premiums collected in a given year. This approach allows insurers to make an operating profit by using investment income to offset those loss amounts that exceed collected premium amounts.

SUMMARY

The concepts of risk, transfer, and pooling are critical components of the insurance mechanism. These three concepts form a foundation on which the insurance mechanism is based.

Premiums collected from all policyholders are pooled to pay the losses of a relative few policyholders. It is important for insurers to make accurate predictions of expected future losses in order to charge each policyholder an appropriate premium. The law of large numbers assists insurers in making reliable estimates of anticipated future loss amounts to determine each individual policyholder's contribution to the pool.

Many types of insurance policies cover personal and commercial loss exposures. The loss exposures of individuals and families are mainly related to their residences, personal vehicles, or owned watercraft. The common types of personal insurance policies are, therefore, homeowners, personal auto policies (PAP), and watercraft policies.

Commercial insurance policies include commercial property coverage, commercial crime, and commercial general liability (CGL) coverage. These coverages are often combined into a single commercial package policy (CPP) or a businessowners policy (BOP). Other common commercial insurance policies include commercial auto, workers compensation, and commercial umbrella.

Insurance provides many benefits to society as a whole and to individuals and businesses. The primary benefit is that insurance provides a mechanism to pay for the financial consequences of losses. Also, because insurance allows for the payment of losses, a related benefit is the reduction of uncertainty regarding how losses, particularly large loss amounts, will be paid. Other benefits of insurance include using resources efficiently, promoting loss control, satisfying legal requirements, and providing a basis for credit.

Every year, insurers collect large amounts of premium dollars from their customers. In return, the insurers promise to pay for any future losses covered under the policies. In addition to using premiums to pay losses, insurers must also pay expenses related to paying claims and operating the business. Insurers also invest funds that are not immediately needed to pay losses or expenses.

Direct Your Learning

Insurance Marketing

Educational Objectives

After learning the content of this chapter and completing the corresponding course guide assignment, you should be able to:

- Identify the parties to an insurance transaction and the role of each.
- Identify insurance producer job functions and the purpose of each.
- Contrast the common insurance marketing systems in terms of the following:
  - Their contractual relationship with insurers
  - Their method of compensation
  - Their ownership of expirations

Outline

The Insurance Transaction

Producer Functions

Insurance Marketing Systems

Summary

Insurance Marketing

THE INSURANCE TRANSACTION

An insurance transaction occurs when a customer purchases insurance either directly from an insurer or through a producer.

Most insurance transactions involve at least two parties: an insured (policyholder) and an insurance company, or insurer. Many other insurance transactions may include a third party, the producer. Producers are involved in the sale of insurance products and include sales representatives, agents, and brokers.

Insured

Property-casualty insurers sell insurance to two broad groups of customers: individuals and families and for-profit and not-for-profit organizations. Individuals and families purchase **personal insurance** to insure their non-business exposures. The two major types of personal insurance policies are homeowners and personal auto policies.

The property-casualty insurance needs of businesses are generally more complex than those of individuals and families. For-profit organizations and not-for-profit organizations (such as educational, religious, and governmental entities) purchase commercial insurance to insure their loss exposures. Commercial loss exposures are those that affect an organization's operation—for example, damage to business property from loss due to fire or vandalism, work-related injuries to employees, liability for injuries to customers, liability for injuries to others caused by the use of autos, and damage to the insured's own autos.

Because the insured is the party protected by an insurance policy, every insurance policy names at least one insured. However, property and liability policies can also include coverage for parties other than those named insureds. For example, under a homeowners policy, coverage is provided for family members who reside in the home of the individual or couple who are named insureds.

Insurer

The second party to the insurance transaction is the insurer. Prospective insureds complete insurance applications, which are submitted to one or more insurers. The insurer's staff reviews these applications to determine whether

> **Personal insurance**
> Insurance that covers the financial consequences of losses to individuals and families caused by death, illness, injury, disability, and unemployment.

the characteristics of the customer match the insurer's eligibility and selection guidelines. If so, the insurer accepts the exposures of the insured and issues an insurance policy for that customer. If the customer's characteristics do not meet the insurer's guidelines, the insurer will decline to provide coverage, and the customer must then seek insurance coverage with another insurer.

Insurers also collect premiums, pay covered losses, and provide ongoing customer service, such as processing endorsements, providing loss control services, and responding to billing questions.

Leading Writers of Property-Casualty Insurance by Direct Premiums Written, 2005

($000)

Rank	Company/Group	Direct premiums written[1]	Market share (percent)
1	State Farm Mutual Group	$48,762,122	10.1%
2	American International Group	35,137,606	7.3
3	Allstate Insurance Co. Group	27,320,402	5.7
4	St. Paul Travelers Companies and Affiliates	21,495,050	4.5
5	Liberty Mutual Group	16,560,115	3.4
6	Nationwide Group	15,251,121	3.2
7	Farmers Insurance Group	14,474,090	3.0
8	Progressive Casualty Group	14,298,029	3.0
9	Zurich Insurance Co. Group	13,487,690	2.8
10	Hartford Fire Group	12,858,226	2.7

[1] Before reinsurance transactions, excluding state funds.

Source: National Association of Insurance Commissioners (NAIC) Annual Statement Database via Highline Data, LLC. Copyrighted information. No portion of this work may be copied or redistributed without the express written permission of Highline Data, LLC.

Producer

A third possible party to the insurance transaction is the **producer**. Many insurance policies are sold through a producer.

A producer may be either an agent or an insurance broker. Producers may work independently, or they may be salaried or commissioned employees or independent contractors of an insurance brokerage firm. An independent agent's organization is called an independent agency, and a broker's organization is called a brokerage. An independent agency or a brokerage can consist of one person working alone, or it can include several agents or brokers

Producer
A person who sells insurance products for one or more insurers.

working with customer service representatives and other specialists. In contrast to an insurance agent or agency, which has a contractual relationship with an insurer, a broker represents the insured in locating insurance coverage and insurers that best meet that customer's needs.

PRODUCER FUNCTIONS

Producers perform many important functions, which vary from one producer to another.

Generally, the functions that insurance producers are to perform are specified in the agency or brokerage contract. These functions vary widely from one producer to another and depend on the size of the producer's firm, the types of customers, and the complexity of accounts the producer handles. These are a producer's typical functions:

- Prospecting
- Risk management review
- Sales
- Policy issuance
- Premium collection
- Customer service
- Claim handling

Some producers perform all of these functions, while others perform only some of them.

Prospecting

Prospecting involves locating persons, businesses, and other entities that might be interested in purchasing the insurance products and services offered by the insurer or companies the producer represents. Prospects can be located using one of these methods:

- Referrals from present clients
- Referrals from strategic partners (such as banks, real estate brokers, and so on)
- Advertising and direct mail
- Interactive Web sites
- Telephone solicitations and cold calls

The producer is typically responsible for his or her own prospecting. However, large agencies and brokerages may have employees who specialize in locating prospective clients.

Risk Management Review

Another function producers perform is risk management review. Risk management review is the principal method used to determine a prospect's insurance needs. For an individual or a family, the risk management review process can be relatively simple, requiring the completion of an interview or a questionnaire that assists in identifying the prospect's loss exposures and it enables the producer to suggest methods—often insurance-based—for treating them. Because the loss exposures of a business are more complex, the risk management review process for businesses is also likely to be more complex. A substantial amount of the producer's time is required to develop and analyze loss exposure information for a large firm with diversified operations and/or multiple locations.

Sales

Selling insurance products and services is one of the most important functions of an insurance producer because sales are essential to sustaining the livelihood of the agency or brokerage. Commission on policy premiums produced is the principal source of income for producers and the agencies or brokerages for which they work. Steps in the sales process include contacting the prospective client, determining the prospect's needs, preparing and presenting a proposal, closing the sale, issuing binders if necessary, and providing initial customer service.

Policy Issuance

Another function some producers perform is policy issuance. Some producers maintain a supply of an insurer's pre-printed policies and forms in their offices and issue them as needed to their customers, while other producers use their own agency management systems to generate computer-issued policies on site. More common is insurers' practice of assembling policies at the producer's request and either mailing them directly to policyholders or sending them to the producer for delivery to the insured.

Premium Collection

Producers who issue policies might also prepare policy invoices and collect premiums. The **agency bill** process may be used for personal insurance policies, but it is more commonly used with large commercial accounts. For small commercial accounts and the majority of personal insurance, the insured is usually directed to send premium payments to the insurer, bypassing the producer in a procedure known as the **direct bill** process.

Agency bill
A payment procedure in which a producer sends premium bills to the insured, collects the premium, and sends the premium to the insurer, less any applicable commission.

Direct bill
A payment procedure in which an insurer sends premium bills to the insured, collects the premium, and sends any commission payable on the premium collected to the producer.

Customer Service

Most producers are involved in customer service to some degree and offer value-added services and personalize insurance packages to differentiate them from their competitors in the marketplace. As another example of customer service, the producer might take an endorsement request over the phone, quote a price for additional coverages, or transfer a customer who has had a loss to the claim department.

Additional customer service functions that producers perform include responding to billing inquiries, performing customer account reviews, and engaging in field underwriting (obtaining loss reports, insurance credit scores, motor vehicle reports, and so on). Producers must be able to respond to questions about policyholders' existing coverage and additional coverage requirements. Finally, producers are expected to facilitate contacts between policyholders and insurer personnel, including premium auditors and loss control representatives.

Claim Handling

All producers are likely to be involved to some extent in handling claims made by their policyholders. Because the producer is the policyholder's principal contact with the insurer, many insureds naturally call the producer first when a claim occurs.

In some cases, the producer may simply give the policyholder the telephone number of the insurer's claim department and possibly the name of a person to speak with. Alternatively, the producer may obtain some basic information about the claim from the policyholder, relay it to the insurer, and arrange for a claim representative to contact the insured. Frequently, insurers issue their policies with a "claim kit" directing their policyholders in the proper procedures and contacts.

Finally, many producers are authorized by their insurers to adjust some types of claims. Most often, the authorization is limited to small first-party property claims—for example, property losses under $5,000. Less frequently, if they are properly trained to do so, some producers are also authorized to settle small third-party liability claims. Usually, these claims are for auto property damage liability losses. A few large agencies or brokerages that employ skilled claim personnel might be authorized to settle large, more complex claims. The limitations on the producer's claim-handling authority should be specified in the agency contract.

Claim handling by qualified producers offers two major advantages: quicker service to policyholders and lower loss adjustment expenses to the insurer. However, if the producer is not properly trained in how to handle claims, overpayment of claims might offset the savings.

INSURANCE MARKETING SYSTEMS

Producers often market and sell insurance to consumers within three marketing systems:

- Independent agency and brokerage marketing system
- Exclusive agency marketing system
- Direct writer marketing system

These systems differ based on specific characteristics:

- Contractual relationship with insurers
- Method of compensation
- Ownership of expirations

Independent Agency and Brokerage Marketing System

Independent agency and brokerage marketing system
An insurance marketing system under which producers (agents or brokers), who are independent contractors, sell insurance, usually as representatives of several unrelated insurers.

Producers in the **independent agency and brokerage marketing system** are not employees of any insurer and are usually free to work with as many insurers as they want. They sell insurance products to individuals and businesses and provide policy services, such as analyzing customers' insurance needs, explaining and recommending various coverages, and completing the insurance application. Producers may also assist insurers in handling claims made by the producer's customers. A producer's claim assistance may consist of collecting loss information, submitting claims to the insurer, or actually settling small claims.

A broker is similar to an agent in that the broker also sells insurance products to individuals and businesses and provides policy services. However, the broker represents the prospective insured, while the agent represents the insurer. A broker locates insurance policies—from all insurers—that best meet the consumer's needs and provides the same policy services that independent agencies provide.

Insurers pay independent agents and brokers a commission, typically a percentage of the premium, for each policy sold. Commission rates might vary for new and renewal business and by type of policy.

Independent agents and brokers own the policy expirations, which are the record of present policyholders and the dates their policies expire. Because they own the policy expirations, independent agents and brokers can place business with any of the insurers they represent or through any producers who have access to insurers that the primary producer does not. An independent agent's ownership of expirations is usually clearly stated in the agency contract. Although a broker does not have agency contracts with the insurers it represents, a broker's (or an agent's) ownership of expirations exists as a matter of custom and law even in the absence of a contract provision. The expirations are usually the largest and most marketable asset of an insurance agency or brokerage.

If an independent agent does not renew its contract with a particular insurer, the agent can place the policies written by that insurer with another insurer. Brokers, in contrast, have no contract with any insurer and are always free to place business with other insurers. An agent or a broker also has the right to sell its expiration list to another independent agent or broker. If the agency or brokerage were to be sold, for example, the buyer would want to keep the previous owner's customers and would need the expiration list to solicit those customers.

Exclusive Agency Marketing System

The **exclusive agency marketing system** uses independent contractors called exclusive agents, who represent only one insurer or a group of related insurers, possibly under common ownership. Like independent agents, exclusive agents are independent contractors and are not employees of an insurer. But in contrast to independent agents, most exclusive agents have contracts that prohibit them from selling insurance for any other insurer.

The insurer often handles many administrative functions for the exclusive agency. These functions include policy issuance, premium collection, and claim processing. Exclusive agents might offer some claim handling services similar to those offered by independent agents and brokers.

Exclusive agents are usually paid commissions, and the commission percentage is sometimes higher for new business than it is for renewal business. Exclusive agents may also receive a bonus for exceeding sales goals. Unlike independent agents, exclusive agents do not own the policy expirations; the insurer does. Therefore, if an exclusive agent does not renew its agency contract with the insurer, the insurer retains control of the policies written by the exclusive agent.

Exclusive agency marketing system
An insurance marketing system under which agents contract to sell insurance exclusively for one insurer (or for an associated group of insurers).

Direct Writer Marketing System

The **direct writer marketing system** is similar to the exclusive agency system in that the sales representatives used by the insurer are restricted to representing only that insurer or a group of insurers under common ownership and management. However, in contrast to an exclusive agent, a direct writer agent is employed by the insurer and receives a salary, a bonus, a commission, or a combination of the three.

Because direct writer agents are employees of the insurers they represent, they do not have any ownership of expirations. Like exclusive agents, agents for direct writers are largely free of responsibility for administrative functions, which are handled by the insurer.

Direct writer marketing system
An insurance marketing system that uses sales agents (or sales representatives) who are direct employees of the insurer.

Differences Among Insurance Marketing Systems

Type of Marketing System	Contractual Relationship With Insurers	Method of Compensation	Ownership of Expirations	Insurers Represented
Independent agency and brokerage marketing system	Independent contractors (not employees of insurer)	Sales commissions	Producer owns expirations	Usually more than one insurer
Exclusive agency marketing system	Independent contractors (not employees of insurer)	Sales commissions and bonus	Insurer owns expirations	Only one insurer
Direct writer marketing system	Employees of insurer	Salary, bonus, sales commissions, or a combination	Insurer owns expirations	Only the producer's employer

SUMMARY

The insurance transaction involves at least two parties: the insured and the insurer. In some cases, a producer is included as a third party to the insurance transaction. The insured can be either an individual or a family who purchases personal insurance, or a not-for-profit or for-profit organization that purchases commercial insurance. The insurer accepts the loss exposures of the insureds according to its selection guidelines. The producer, who can be either an agent or a broker, sells insurance products for one or more insurers.

An insurance producer's typical functions vary widely from one producer to another and depend on the size of the producer's firm, the types of customers, and the complexity of accounts the producer handles. Producers typically engage in prospecting, risk management review, and sales activities. In addition, they issue policies, prepare policy invoices, and collect premiums, using either the agency bill or direct bill process. Producers also participate in customer service, usually by providing value-added services and personalized insurance packages. Finally, producers often help insureds with claim handling, either by providing helpful information or settling the insured's claim directly.

Insurance marketing systems consist of the independent agency and brokerage marketing system, the exclusive agency marketing system, and the direct writer marketing system. These three marketing systems can be contrasted based on the following characteristics of the agents or brokers used by each system: their contractual relationship with the insurers whose policies they sell, their method of compensation, and their ownership of expirations.

Direct Your Learning

Insurance Services

Educational Objectives

After learning the content of this chapter and completing the corresponding course guide assignment, you should be able to:

- Categorize property-casualty insurers on the basis of their classifications and types.
- Identify the roles of the following insurer functions:
  - Marketing
  - Underwriting
  - Claims
  - Loss control
  - Premium audit
- Explain why and how insurance operations are regulated.

Outline

Classifications and Types of Insurers

Insurer Functions

Insurance Regulation

Summary

Insurance Services

CLASSIFICATIONS AND TYPES OF INSURERS

Insurers can be classified by form of ownership, place of incorporation, licensing status, and by marketing system.

It is important for insurance professionals to be familiar with the different forms of ownership of insurance companies, how to classify insurers by where they are incorporated, what gives them the legal authority to operate in a particular state, and how they sell their policies. Insurance professionals must be able to distinguish between the different types of insurers in order to assess which type of insurer is most appropriate for their customers.

Form of Ownership

Insurers can be classified by legal form of ownership. These are the major forms of insurer ownership:

- Stock insurance companies
- Mutual insurance companies
- Reciprocal insurance exchanges
- Lloyds
- Captive insurance companies
- Reinsurance companies
- Government insurers

Stock Insurance Companies

Insurers formed for the purpose of making a profit for their owners are typically organized as **stock insurers**. For-profit corporations are owned by their stockholders. By purchasing stock in a for-profit insurer, stockholders supply the capital needed to form the insurance company or the additional capital the insurer needs to expand its operations. Stockholders expect to receive a return on their investment in the form of stock dividends, increased stock value, or both.

Stockholders have the right to elect the board of directors, which has the authority to control the insurer's activities. The board of directors creates and oversees corporate goals and objectives and appoints a chief executive officer (CEO) to carry out the insurer's operations and implement the programs necessary to operate the company.

Stock insurer
An insurer that is owned by its stockholders and formed as a corporation for the purpose of earning a profit for the stockholders.

Mutual Insurance Companies

A **mutual insurer** is a corporation owned by its policyholders. Because a traditional mutual insurer issues no common stock, it has no stockholders. Its policyholders have voting rights similar to those of a stock company's stockholders, and, like stockholders, they elect the insurer's board of directors. Mutual companies include some large national insurers and many regional insurers.

Although initially formed to provide insurance for their owners, mutual insurers today generally seek to earn profits in their ongoing operations, just as stock companies do. A mutual insurer needs profits to ensure the future financial health of the organization.

Reciprocal Insurance Exchanges

A **reciprocal insurance exchange**, also simply called a reciprocal, consists of a series of private contracts in which **subscribers**, or members of the group, agree to insure each other. The term "reciprocal" comes from the reciprocity of responsibility of all subscribers to each other. Each member of the reciprocal is both an insured and an insurer. Because the subscribers are not experts in running an insurance operation, they contract with an individual or organization to operate the reciprocal; this manager is called an **attorney-in-fact**. The subscribers empower the attorney-in-fact to handle all the duties necessary to manage the reciprocal. An insurer may be formed as a reciprocal in order to receive favorable tax treatment.

Lloyds

Among the forms of insurance ownership is a unique form known as Lloyds. Two types of Lloyds associations exist: Lloyd's of London and American Lloyds.

Lloyd's of London (Lloyd's) is technically not an insurance company. However, it does provide the physical and procedural facilities for its members to write insurance. It is a marketplace, similar to a stock exchange. The members are investors who hope to earn a profit from the insurance operations.

Each individual investor (called a "Name") of Lloyd's belongs to one or more groups called syndicates. A syndicate's underwriter or group of underwriters assesses applications for insurance coverage. Depending on the nature and amount of insurance requested, the underwriters for a syndicate might accept all or a portion of the total amount of insurance. If they accept only a portion, the application is forwarded to another syndicate to solicit its acceptance of a portion or the full remainder of the coverage needed. For example, if the owners of a large commercial office building want to insure the value of the building against a loss caused by fire, they may have to approach several syndicates to obtain enough coverage to replace the entire building if a complete loss were to occur.

Mutual insurer
An insurer that is owned by its policyholders and formed as a corporation for the purpose of providing insurance to them.

Reciprocal insurance exchange
An insurer owned by its policyholders, formed as an unincorporated association for the purpose of providing insurance coverage to its members (called subscribers), and managed by an attorney-in-fact.

Subscribers
The policyholders of a reciprocal insurance exchange who agree to insure each other.

Attorney-in-fact
In a reciprocal insurance exchange, the contractually authorized manager of the reciprocal who administers its affairs and carries out its insurance transactions.

The insurance written by each Name is backed by his or her entire personal fortune. However, each Name is liable only for the insurance he or she agrees to write, not for the obligations assumed by any other Name

American Lloyds associations are smaller than Lloyd's of London, and most are domiciled in Texas. Most were formed or have been acquired by insurance companies. Unlike the individual Names of Lloyd's of London, members (called underwriters) of American Lloyds are not liable beyond their investment in the association.

Captive Insurance Companies

When a business organization or a group of affiliated organizations forms a subsidiary company to provide all or part of their insurance, the subsidiary is known as a **captive insurer**, or simply a **captive**. This arrangement is sometimes referred to as "formalized self-insurance." For example, a large retail chain may decide it can insure itself at a more reasonable cost by using a captive rather than an unaffiliated insurance company. The captive may also be formed to cover losses that other insurers will not cover at any price.

Reinsurance Companies

Some private insurers provide **reinsurance**, a contractual arrangement that transfers some or all of the potential costs of insured losses from policies written by one insurer to another insurer. The insurer that transfers the loss exposures is the **primary insurer** (also called the reinsured), and the insurer that accepts the loss exposures is the **reinsurer**. Primary insurers use reinsurance to transfer loss exposures that may result in losses beyond their ability to pay. For example, if an insurer sells homeowners policies in a geographic area that is subject to hurricanes or tornadoes, many of its customers could be simultaneously affected by a single weather event. Such an event would therefore require the insurer to pay a substantial amount for losses for this single event. If the insurer has a reinsurance agreement in place, it would share the financial burden of paying such losses with the reinsurer, which would lessen the financial impact for the primary insurer. Some reinsurers are companies or organizations that specialize in the reinsurance business. Other reinsurers are also primary insurers.

Government Insurers

Despite the size and diversity of private insurers in the United States, private insurers do not provide some types of insurance. Some loss exposures, such as catastrophic flooding, do not possess the characteristics that make them commercially insurable, but a significant need for protection against the potential losses still exists. Both the federal government and state governments have developed insurance programs to meet specific insurance needs of the public. Some federal government insurance programs serve the public in a manner that only the government can. For example, only the government has the

Captive insurer, or captive
A subsidiary formed to insure the loss exposures of its parent company and the parent's affiliates.

Reinsurance
The transfer of insurance risk from one insurer to another through a contractual agreement under which one insurer (the reinsurer) agrees, in return for a reinsurance premium, to indemnify another insurer (the primary insurer) for some or all of the financial consequences of certain loss exposures covered by the primary's insurance policies.

Primary insurer
The insurer that transfers or cedes all or part of the insurance risk it has assumed to another insurer.

Reinsurer
The insurer that assumes some or all of the potential costs of insured loss exposures of the primary insurer in a reinsurance contractual agreement.

ability to tax in order to provide the financial resources needed to insure some of the larger loss exposures.

The federal government offers several forms of insurance. One of the largest property insurance programs it offers is the National Flood Insurance Program (NFIP), which is administered by the Federal Insurance Administration under the Federal Emergency Management Agency. Most property insurance policies exclude flood coverage because the catastrophic loss potential of floods would significantly raise property insurance premiums for all customers. Customers located in an area prone to flooding can obtain the needed coverage through the NFIP program.

All states offer some form of government insurance. For example, some states provide workers compensation insurance for some or all employers in the state. Most state workers compensation programs compete with private insurers. However, in some states, workers compensation insurance is offered exclusively by the state.

Hurricane-Damaged Home

Residual market
The term referring collectively to insurers and other organizations that make insurance available through a shared risk mechanism to those who cannot obtain coverage in the admitted market.

Most states require motor vehicle owners to have auto liability insurance before registering their vehicles. However, drivers with poor driving records or with little driving experience may have difficulty obtaining insurance from private insurers. To make liability insurance available to almost all licensed drivers, all states have implemented automobile insurance plans through a **residual market**. The cost of operating such plans is spread among all private insurers selling auto insurance in the state.

In most states, Fair Access to Insurance Requirements (FAIR) plans make property insurance more readily available to property owners who have exposures to loss over which they have no control, such as being in a neighborhood with a high property crime rate. These state-run plans spread the cost of operating the plan among all private insurers selling property insurance in the state. Without such a program, individuals and business owners located in such areas who have exposures to loss over which they have no control would be unable to obtain property insurance for their buildings or contents.

Beachfront and windstorm insurance pools are residual market plans similar to FAIR plans. These plans, available in states along the Atlantic and Gulf Coasts, provide insurance to property owners who are unable to obtain this coverage from private insurers. The plans provide coverage for wind damage from hurricanes and other windstorms.

Place of Incorporation

Insurers can be classified by place of incorporation as domestic, foreign, or alien insurers. Insurance is regulated at the state level. Therefore, a **domestic insurer** is one incorporated within a specific state or, if not incorporated, formed under the laws of that state. An insurer is said to be operating in its own domiciled state when it is doing business in the state in which it is incorporated or formed.

Reciprocal exchanges are the only unincorporated insurers permitted in most states. Insurance exchanges and Lloyds organizations are permitted under law in only a few states. A **foreign insurer** is a domestic insurer that is licensed to do business in states other than its domiciled state. **Alien insurers** are incorporated or formed in another country.

Licensing Status

Another way to classify insurers is by licensing status. An insurer's state license authorizes it to sell insurance in the state. A license indicates that the insurer has met the state's minimum standards for financial strength, competence, and integrity. If the insurer later fails to meet those standards or fails to comply with a state law, regulation, or rule, its license can be revoked.

A **licensed insurer**, or **admitted insurer**, is an insurer that has been granted a license to operate in a particular state. An **unlicensed insurer**, or **nonadmitted insurer** has not been granted a license to operate. Producers who sell insurance are licensed to place business only with admitted insurers. Producers can sell insurance of nonadmitted insurers, but only after licensed insurers have declined to write it and only if the producer has a special license to sell **excess and surplus lines (E&S) insurance**.

Domestic insurer
An insurer doing business in its home state.

Foreign insurer
An insurer licensed to operate in a state but incorporated in another state.

Alien insurer
An insurer licensed in a U.S. state but incorporated in another country.

Licensed insurer, or **admitted insurer**
An insurer authorized by the state insurance department to sell insurance within that state.

Unlicensed insurer, or **nonadmitted insurer**
An insurer not authorized by the state insurance department to transact business in the insured's state.

Excess and surplus lines (E&S) insurance
Insurance coverages unavailable in the standard market that are written by nonadmitted insurers.

Marketing Systems

Marketing system
The system that directs and facilitates the design, development, sale, and support of a product or service.

Insurers can also be classified by **marketing system**—that is, the system used to deliver insurance products to the marketplace. Insurers use many types of marketing systems, also known as distribution channels, designed to meet their particular marketing objectives. Most insurers use one or more of these marketing systems:

- Independent agency and brokerage system
- Exclusive agency system
- Direct writer system
- Alternative distribution channels

Independent Agency and Brokerage System

Insurance sales in the independent agency and brokerage system are made through independent insurance agents. The agency can be organized as a sole proprietorship (owned by an individual), a partnership (owned by two or more individuals), or a corporation (owned by stockholders).

Agency expiration list
The record of an insurance agency's present policyholders and the dates their policies expire.

A distinguishing feature of the independent agency systems is the ownership of the **agency expiration list**. The typical independent agency contract specifies that the independent agency—not the insurer—owns the list of policyholders, the dates their existing policies expire, and, most importantly, the right to solicit these policyholders for insurance. The policyholders are free to choose another agency or insurer. However, another agency representing the same insurer cannot solicit the policyholder. The exclusive right to solicit policyholders is a valuable asset that can be sold.

Insurance broker
An independent business owner or firm (or an employee of such a firm) that sells insurance by representing customers rather than insurers.

Closely related to and often working with independent agencies are **insurance brokers**. Unlike independent agents, the broker is working for the insurance buyer, rather than the insurer. Brokers shop among insurers to find the best coverage or value for their clients, the insurance buyers.

In practice, despite the technical distinctions between brokers and independent agents, the differences are quite limited. Both brokers and independent agents are intermediaries between insurers and insurance buyers, and both collect premiums from insureds and remit them to insurers. Both are in the business of finding people with insurance needs and selling insurance appropriate to those needs. In fact, some states have eliminated the difference in their licenses and simply refer to them collectively as producers.

Exclusive Agency System

Exclusive agent
An agent that has a contract to sell insurance exclusively for one insurer or a group of related insurers.

An **exclusive agent**, like the independent agent, owns his or her own insurance sales agency. However, the exclusive agency system limits the agent to selling insurance exclusively for one insurer or group of related companies. If a desired type of insurance is not written by the insurer represented, some contracts allow the agent to place ("broker") the business with an independent agent or another exclusive agent.

Generally, an exclusive agent is not an employee of the insurer but a self-employed representative of the company. Further, the expiration list belongs not to the exclusive agent but to the insurer, which can use the customer information as a source of prospects for follow-up sales by its other exclusive agents.

Direct Writer System

As with the exclusive agency system, agents in the direct writer marketing system sell insurance for only one insurer or group. Agents in the direct writer system are employees of the insurer, and their job is to sell insurance for the company. Employees who work as insurance producers for a direct writer are generally called sales representatives.

The direct writer's sales representative is an employee of the insurer. Further, the expiration list belongs not to the sales representative but to the insurer, which can use the customer information as it would in an exclusive agency system.

Alternative Distribution Channels

In addition to these three more traditional marketing systems, insurers or producers also use these alternative distribution channels to sell insurance:

- Direct response
- Internet
- Call centers
- Group marketing
- Financial institutions

The **direct response distribution channel** markets directly to customers. No producer is used. Although this distribution channel is also called direct mail, customers can contact insurers via the Internet or telephone, not just by mail. Direct response relies heavily on advertising and targeting specific groups of affiliated customers.

> **Direct response distribution channel**
> An insurance distribution channel that markets directly to the customer through such distribution channels as mail, telephone, or the Internet.

The Internet is another alternative distribution channel. The Internet can be used by all parties to the insurance transaction: the insurer, the producer, and the customer. Customers can interact with insurers via Internet-based insurance distributors, also called insurance portals or aggregators. These portals deliver potential customers' contact information to the insurers whose products they offer through their Web sites.

Call centers are also alternative distributions channels. The best-equipped call centers can replicate many of the activities of producers. In addition to making product sales, call center staff can respond to general inquiries, handle claim processing, answer billing questions, and process policy endorsements.

Group marketing sells insurance products and services to individuals or businesses that are members in the same organization, profession, or age group. The members could also be affiliated by their similar interests or hobbies.

Insurers and producers can also elect to market their products and services through a financial institution. Marketing arrangements can range from a small insurance agency placing an agent at a desk in a local bank to a large insurer forming a strategic alliance with a national financial holding company to solicit customers.

INSURER FUNCTIONS

Insurers perform many functions to provide products and services to their customers.

Insurers sell insurance policies and pay claims as required by those policies, but they do much more. They perform multiple key functions in order to accomplish their goal of protecting their customers while earning a profit:

- Marketing
- Underwriting
- Claims
- Loss control
- Premium audit

Many insurers have a department for each of these functions. Some insurers may outsource some functions, and others combine several functions within a department. Insurers may use different terms for these functions than those used here.

Each of these functions contribute to or detract from the overall effectiveness of the insurer, depending on how well it is performed. The functions must also interact with each other; their efficient interaction is vital to the survival and continued success of an insurer.

Marketing

Marketing involves determining the products or services customers want and need and delivering them to those customers. The marketing function contributes significantly to an insurer's profit goals and its goals of meeting customers' needs. The insurer cannot make a profit if it does not provide products and services the customer needs.

An insurer will likely include these elements in a successful marketing program:

- Using market research to determine the needs of potential customers
- Advertising to inform customers about the insurer's products and services
- Training to prepare the sales force to meet the customer's needs

- Setting sales goals and implementing strategies for achieving them
- Motivating and managing the sales force

Underwriting

The role of the underwriting function is to determine what loss exposures will be insured, for what amount of coverage, at what price, and under what conditions. The purpose of **underwriting** is to develop and maintain a profitable **book of business** for the insurer. A book of business is all of the policies that an insurer has in force or some subgroup of those policies. For example, a book of business can include all of an insurer's homeowners policies or all of its auto policies. The term "book of business" can also refer to business produced in a specific geographic area or by a particular branch office. Underwriters typically follow the underwriting process, which involves gathering the necessary information, making the underwriting decision, and implementing the underwriting decision.

The process of making the underwriting decision involves these activities:

- Selecting insureds
- Pricing coverage
- Determining policy terms and conditions
- Monitoring underwriting decisions

Selecting Insureds

Underwriters carefully screen potential insureds to determine which ones to insure. They make their selections by applying the underwriting criteria set by the insurer to the loss exposures of customers who have applied for insurance policies. A successful underwriting function ensures that those applicants who are selected receive the level of coverage that adequately reflects their loss exposures at the appropriate price.

Insurers try to select insureds whose covered losses are not likely to exceed the amount the insurer anticipated when it set the price for the coverage. Underwriters minimize **adverse selection** by screening applicants to avoid those who present loss potentials not adequately reflected in the price being charged.

An example of adverse selection involves houses along a river that occasionally floods. The owners of the homes near the river are more likely to seek out and purchase flood insurance than those who own a house on a hill.

Pricing Coverage

After selecting insureds, underwriting determines the price for the insurance. The goal is to charge a premium that is commensurate with the loss exposure. In other words, each insured's premium should be set at a level that is adequate to enable the total premiums paid by a large group of similar insureds to

> **Underwriting**
> The process of selecting insureds, pricing coverage, determining insurance policy terms and conditions, and then monitoring the underwriting decisions made.
>
> **Book of business**
> A group of policies with a common characteristic, such as territory or type of coverage, or all policies written by a particular insurer or agency.
>
> **Adverse selection**
> In general, the tendency for people with the greatest probability of loss to be the ones most likely to purchase insurance.

pay the losses and expenses of that group and to allow the insurer to achieve a reasonable profit.

The premium is determined by estimating the probability that a loss will occur, the probable severity of a loss if it occurs, and the value of what the insured wants to protect from loss.

Determining Policy Terms and Conditions

Selection of insureds and pricing of coverage are intertwined with a third underwriting activity—determining policy terms and conditions, which require certain circumstances to occur or not occur before coverage will apply to a loss. An insurer must decide exactly what policy terms and conditions of coverage it will offer each applicant. For example, an auto insurer may require an insured to agree that coverage will not apply if a loss occurs when the insured vehicle is operated by a certain underage driver.

Standard form
A policy form that contains standard insurance wording; it is used by insurers that subscribe to the services of insurance advisory organizations.

Because many insureds have the same coverage needs, they can use the same insurance policy forms. **Standard forms** containing common policy terms and conditions have been developed by insurance advisory organizations. They are available to insurers that subscribe to (pay for) the organizations' services. Because many insurers use standard forms, policies issued by competing insurers may be identical. However, as common as standard forms have become, some insurers still use their own forms.

For each type of insurance it handles, an insurer needs to decide whether to use standard forms developed by the advisory organizations or to develop its own policy language, possibly providing coverages that differ in some ways from coverages provided by other insurers. For some types of insurance, such as professional liability insurance for physicians or lawyers, there is no standard form, and coverages can differ significantly among those policies.

Monitoring Underwriting Decisions

Hazard
A condition that increases the frequency or severity of a loss.

Monitoring underwriting decisions is an ongoing activity. Underwriting decisions involve an assessment of loss potential. The loss potential for specific insureds depends on various factors, such as **hazards**, loss history, and other conditions specific to an insured. These factors can change over time; therefore, the underwriter must periodically monitor the insured to detect any changes that might affect the insured's loss potential.

An increase in hazards can change an acceptable insured into an unacceptable one for the coverage and premium charged. For example, if an insured converts a garage into a laboratory for producing toxic chemicals, the coverage and premium must be changed to reflect the increase in hazard, or continued coverage might be denied. Monitoring helps underwriters discover such changes and alter coverage and premium as necessary.

Claims

Insurers expect to pay claims. Without claims, insurance would be unnecessary. When policyholders purchase insurance, they are buying protection for the potential financial consequences of covered losses. The insurer promises to make payments to or on behalf of the insured for covered losses. The claim function is responsible for keeping this promise to the insured by providing prompt and professional loss adjustment services.

Because more than half of what insurers spend goes to the claim function, its proper and efficient performance is important to an insurer's profitability. When evaluating a claim, the adjuster typically applies a claim handling process that includes six activities:

1. Acknowledging a claim and assigning it to a claim representative
2. Identifying the policy
3. Contacting the insured or the insured's representative
4. Investigating and documenting the claim
5. Determining cause of loss and loss amount
6. Concluding the claim

The purpose of the claim handling process is to achieve a fair and equitable settlement based on the circumstances of the loss. Loss settlements that are too high increase the cost of insurance for everybody. Loss settlements that are too low deprive the insured of the full benefits of the insurance policy. Paying inadequate loss settlements also diminishes the insurer's business reputation and can negatively affect the marketing function.

Loss Control

The primary purpose of an insurer's loss control function is to prevent or reduce losses, if possible. From an economic viewpoint, controlling losses is preferable to insuring losses because it reduces the waste of valuable resources. As a practical matter, both insuring and controlling losses are likely to be used jointly for most large loss exposures, because preventing all losses is seldom possible.

The loss control function supports underwriters in selecting which loss exposures to insure. Loss control representatives can provide information to underwriters beyond what the application provides. For example, field inspection reports on an applicant's premises and operations can provide important details about the applicant's loss exposures that are not apparent on the application

An insurer's loss control representatives not only serve as the underwriter's eyes and ears, but also provide a valuable service for insureds by helping them prevent losses or reduce their effect. For example, a loss control representative can provide expert advice concerning sprinkler systems for fire suppression.

Premium Audit

Premium audit
Methodical examination of a policyholder's operations, records, and books of account to determine the actual exposure units and premium for insurance coverages already provided.

Another insurer function is the **premium audit** function. Many commercial insurance policies are written subject to audit because the premium amount is based on a loss exposure amount that is unpredictable at the start of the policy period. The purpose of the audit, which occurs at the end of a policy period, is to determine any adjustments to the premium that may be required based the insured's actual loss exposures during that period.

For example, the premium of a workers compensation policy that pays when an employee is injured on the job is based on the size of the employer's loss exposures, which, for workers compensation, is the amount of its payroll. However, due to new hires, raises, terminations, and retirements during the policy period, the employer won't know the actual size of its payroll until the end of the policy period. It is only after the policy period is over that the insurer and the insured are able to determine how much the premium should be.

The insured pays an estimated premium at the beginning of the policy period. At the end of the policy period, typically one year, a premium auditor examines, or audits, the insured's records to determine the final premium. In conducting a premium audit, the auditor examines the insured's records to determine how extensive the insured's operations were. If they were more extensive than estimated, an additional premium is charged. If less extensive, the insured receives a partial refund.

Because of their direct contact with policyholders, premium auditors also have an opportunity to refer specific observations to various insurer departments. Auditors can notify underwriters of larger loss exposures than originally contemplated, unacceptable operations, new products, new operations, or financial problems. Premium audit information can also identify marketing opportunities and assist the claim department in adjusting certain types of losses.

INSURANCE REGULATION

When purchasing insurance, consumers may have many questions and concerns about whether the coverage they are purchasing will really protect them. Insurance regulation is meant to address many of these concerns.

Insurance consumers have many concerns regarding the insurance coverage they purchase. These concerns include whether the policy forms give them the coverage they expect and need, whether the price is appropriate, and whether the insurer will have the resources needed to pay losses that may occur months or even years after a policy is purchased. Even experienced businesspeople have bought the wrong insurance for the wrong price or have been left with worthless policies after an insurer became insolvent. To protect individuals, organizations, and entire communities from these kinds of problems, all of the states in the United States have chosen to regulate insurance.

Regulation varies considerably from state to state. However, almost all states focus their regulatory efforts on the same key areas of insurer operations: licensing, insurance rates, insurance policies, market conduct, and insurer solvency.

Why Insurance Operations Are Regulated

Insurers are regulated primarily for three reasons:

- To protect consumers
- To maintain insurer solvency
- To prevent destructive competition

Although these reasons overlap, each is examined separately.

Protect Consumers

Insurance is regulated to protect consumers. Many insurance policies are complex legal documents that may be difficult for some consumers to analyze and understand. Regulators help protect consumers by reviewing insurance policy forms to determine whether they benefit consumers. Regulators can set coverage standards, specify policy language for certain insurance coverages, and disapprove unacceptable policies.

Insurance regulators also protect consumers against fraud and unethical market behavior by insurers and producers, such as selling unnecessary insurance, misrepresenting coverage to make a sale, or refusing to pay legitimate claims.

Regulators try to ensure that insurance is readily available, especially the insurance that is viewed as a necessity. For example, all states try to make personal auto insurance coverage available by restricting the rights of insurers to cancel or refuse to renew personal auto insurance policies.

Maintain Insurer Solvency

Insurance is regulated to maintain insurer **solvency**. Insurance regulators try to maintain and enhance the financial condition of private insurers for several reasons:

- Premiums are paid in advance and the period of protection extends into the future. If an insurer becomes insolvent, future claims might not be paid even though the premium already has been. Consumers may find it difficult to evaluate insurers' financial ability to keep their promises.
- Regulation is needed to protect the public interest. Large numbers of individuals are adversely affected when insurers become insolvent. For example, an unusually large catastrophe that affects a large area can make an insurer's financial ability to pay claims uncertain, such as when Hurricane Andrew struck Florida in 1992, causing seven insurer insolvencies.

Solvency
The ability of an insurer to meet its financial obligations as they become due, even those resulting from insured losses that may be claimed several years in the future.

- Insurers hold substantial funds for the ultimate benefit of policyholders. Government regulation is necessary to safeguard such funds.

Insurers have become insolvent despite regulatory reviews. However, sound regulation minimizes the number of insolvencies.

Prevent Destructive Competition

Insurance is regulated to prevent destructive competition. Regulators are responsible for determining whether insurance rates are adequate. At times, some insurers price their policies too low in an effort to attract customers away from higher-priced competitors. This practice drives down price levels in the whole insurance market. When, as a result, insurance rate levels become inadequate, some insurers may not collect enough money to pay all of their insureds' claims and may become insolvent. Other insurers might lose so much profit that they withdraw from the market or stop writing new business. An insurance shortage can then develop, and individuals and organizations might be unable to obtain the coverage they need. For example, pharmaceutical companies have found it difficult to obtain commercial liability insurance to cover the risk of product defects in the drugs they manufacture, and some municipalities have had to restrict nonessential services, such as recreational programs and Independence Day fireworks displays, because liability coverage has become unavailable.

How Insurance Operations Are Regulated

Insurance regulation focuses primarily on five key areas:

- Licensing
- Insurance rates
- Insurance policies
- Market conduct
- Insurer solvency

Licensing

Most insurance companies must be licensed by the state insurance department before they are authorized to write insurance policies in that state. An insurer's licensing status in any given state may assume any one of several forms: that of a domestic insurer, a foreign insurer or an alien insurer. Licensing standards vary among these several forms. For example, a domestic insurer's license generally has no expiration date. Licenses of a foreign insurer and an alien insurer generally must be renewed annually.

Domestic insurers usually must meet the conditions imposed on corporations engaged in noninsurance activities as well as some additional conditions imposed on insurers. An applicant for a domestic insurer license must apply for a corporate charter and provide specific information:

- The names and addresses of the individual incorporators
- The name of the proposed corporation and the territories and types of insurance it plans to market
- The insurer's total financing, including authorized capital stock (the total number of shares, if any, that a corporation can sell to raise money), and its **policyholders' surplus**

> **Policyholders' surplus**
> An insurer's total admitted assets minus its total liabilities.

The information about capital stock and surplus is important to licensing regulators because it indicates the insurer's financial soundness. A domestic insurer that is also a stock insurer must meet certain minimum capital and surplus requirements, which vary widely by state, amounts, and types of insurance written. A domestic insurer that is also a mutual insurer has no capital derived from the sale of stock. Therefore, the minimum financial requirement applies only to surplus. Most states require mutual insurers to have an initial surplus equal to the minimum capital and surplus requirement for stock insurers writing the same type of insurance.

To be licensed in an additional state (that is, as a foreign insurer), an insurer first must show that it has satisfied the requirements imposed by its home state (its state of domicile, or the state where it is a domestic insurer). A foreign insurer also must generally satisfy the minimum capital, surplus, and other requirements imposed on domestic insurers within the state in which it is seeking to be licensed.

Alien insurers must satisfy the requirements imposed on domestic insurers by the state in which they want to be licensed. Additionally, they must usually establish a branch office in any state and have funds on deposit in the U.S. equal to the minimum capital and surplus required. The funds on deposit are available, if necessary, to pay claims asserted against the alien insurer through the U.S. legal system.

Insurers that are licensed to do business in a state are collectively referred to as admitted insurers. Under special circumstances, nonlicensed insurers, collectively referred to as nonadmitted insurers, may be permitted to sell insurance within a state. A nonadmitted insurer may be an admitted insurer in other states, or it may even be an alien insurer. Nonadmitted insurers are frequently referred to as surplus lines insurers. Surplus lines insurers are usually permitted to sell only insurance that is not readily available from admitted insurers because of specialty, risk, or several other factors. Under **surplus lines laws**, a nonadmitted insurer would be permitted to transact business only through a specially licensed surplus lines producer. The nonadmitted insurer must still meet some of the regulatory requirements of a licensed insurer, but these do not typically include restrictions on rates and policy forms.

> **Surplus lines laws**
> State laws that permit producers with a surplus lines license to write business for an acceptable "nonadmitted insurer when protection from admitted insurers is not available."

In addition to licensing insurers, all states require licensing of certain insurer representatives or employees. Agents, brokers, and claim representatives are often required to pass an examination on insurance laws and practices to earn a license. These examinations, along with continuing education requirements, are an attempt to ensure that these insurance professionals have a minimum level of insurance knowledge.

Insurance Rates

Setting insurance rates is the regulatory area that may receive the most public attention. An insurer must collect sufficient premiums to pay for the insured losses that occur, to cover the insurer's costs of operating, and to allow a reasonable profit.

When deciding to approve or disapprove of a rate requested by an insurer, a state insurance commissioner often considers three major goals, which are to ensure that the rates meet these criteria:

- Adequate—The rates should be high enough to pay all claims and expenses related to those rates, helping maintain insurer solvency.
- Not excessive—Insurers are entitled to a fair return but not to excessive or unreasonable profits.
- Not unfairly discriminatory—An insurer is allowed to discriminate among groups of insureds, but it must be fair and consistent in doing so; insureds with loss exposures that are roughly similar regarding expected losses and expenses should be charged similar rates.

The manner in which a state achieves these three goals is determined in large part by a state's rating laws. Generally, these are the major types of state rating laws:

- **Mandatory rate law**—Insurers are required to use rates as established by regulators/ state agencies.
- **Prior approval law**—Requires pre-approval by regulators.
- **File-and-use law**—Regulators have the authority to disapprove the rates if they cannot be justified.
- **Use-and-file law**—Insurers can change rates and later submit filing information that is subject to regulatory review.
- **Flex rating law**—Insurers are permitted to increase or decrease their rates within the established range without prior approval.
- **Open competition**—Market prices driven by the economic laws of supply and demand, rather than the discretionary acts of regulators, determine the rates and availability. However, insurers might be required to furnish rate schedules and supporting statistical data to regulatory officials, and the state insurance department has the authority to monitor competition and to disapprove rates if necessary. The goals that rates must be adequate, nonexcessive, and not unfairly discriminatory still apply.

Insurance Policies

Another area of insurance regulation involves insurance policies. Because many insurance policies are difficult to interpret and are often sold on a

Mandatory rate law
State law under which insurance rates are set by a state agency or rating bureau and all licensed insurers are required to use those rates.

Prior approval law
State law under which insurance rates must be approved by the state insurance department before they can be used.

File-and-use law
State law under which insurance rates must be filed with the state insurance department but can then be used immediately.

Use-and-file law
An insurance rating law that requires rates to be filed within a specified period after they are first used in the state.

Flex rating law
State law under which prior approval is required only if the new rates exceed a certain percentage above (and sometimes below) the rates previously filed.

Open competition
A system under which rates do not have to be filed with the state insurance department.

take-it-or-leave-it basis, many states require insurers to file their policy forms with the state insurance department in a manner similar to the method used for rate filings.

Regulations relating to policy language are usually for the purpose of ensuring that policies are clear and readable. Regulators may also detect provisions that may be unfair or unreasonable. Although the possibility always exists that an insured might misinterpret a policy, regulatory approval of policy forms reduces the possibility of misleading wording.

Some state legislatures enact laws that control the structure and content of insurance policies. Such laws may require the use of a specific policy form or a provision in all policies of a certain type sold in the state. For example, many states require the use of a standard workers compensation policy, which pays for injuries to employees that occur on the job. Some state laws require all insurance policies to meet a readability test, which, in addition to common, easily understood language, may require a specific policy style, form, and print size.

Market Conduct

Market conduct regulation focuses on insurers' treatment of applicants for insurance, insureds, and others who present claims for coverage. Most states have statutes that address market conduct, often called **unfair trade practices acts**. These acts, which identify certain practices that are considered unfair to the public, usually involve three areas of insurance company operations: sales, underwriting, and claim handling.

State regulators can suspend or revoke the licenses of sales agents or brokers who engage in unfair trade practices, such as embezzling premiums paid. Similarly, an insurer that is guilty of unfair underwriting practices could be fined, or its operating license in a state could be suspended or revoked. Per the unfair trade practices acts, examples of improper underwriting include unfair discrimination and canceling or not renewing policies, contrary to state regulations.

Most states also have statutes that prohibit unfair claim practices and assess fines against claim representatives and insurers that engage in such practices, such as intentionally making unfairly low settlement offers, failing to provide reasonable explanations for denying a claim, misrepresenting important policy provisions, or failing to approve or deny coverage within a reasonable time period.

Regulatory examinations of insurers identify some of the abuses just discussed, but other abuses are exposed only when an insured or a claimant lodges a complaint. Every state insurance department has a consumer complaints division to enforce its consumer protection objectives and to help insureds deal with problems they have encountered with insurers and their representatives. State insurance departments investigate consumer complaints and may hold formal hearings as part of the investigation process.

Market conduct regulation
Regulation of the practices of insurers in regard to four areas of operation: sales practices, underwriting practices, claim practices, and bad-faith actions.

Unfair trade practices act
State law that specifies certain prohibited business practices.

3.20 Introduction to Property and Casualty Insurance

Insurer Solvency

Another area of insurance regulation is insurer solvency. A noninsurance company is considered solvent if it has resources to pay its bills and meet similar financial obligations. Because an insurer has promised to pay many unknown losses in the future, states require it to have financial reserves well in excess of its ordinary expenses in order to be considered solvent. Solvency for an insurer is its ability to meet its financial obligations as they become due, even those resulting from insured losses that might be claimed several years in the future. To verify insurer solvency, insurance regulators conduct **solvency surveillance**, carefully monitoring insurers' financial condition.

Regulators use four methods to verify the solvency of insurers:

- Establish financial requirements by which to measure solvency
- Conduct on-site field examinations to ensure regulatory compliance
- Review annual financial statements
- Administer the Insurance Regulatory Information System (IRIS)

The first method to verify solvency is to establish financial requirements against which all similarly licensed insurers are measured. To obtain and keep a license as an admitted insurer, each insurer must meet certain minimum financial requirements, such as capital and surplus requirements. Specific financial requirements vary widely by state.

The second method to verify solvency is to conduct on-site field examinations. State laws usually require that insurers be examined at least once every three to five years. This examination usually occurs under the direction of the insurance department of the state where the insurer's home office is located. A team of state examiners, working at the insurance company home office, reviews a wide range of activities, including claim, underwriting, marketing, and accounting procedures. Of particular interest to the examiners is the financial condition of the insurer. The financial records of the insurer are carefully analyzed to ensure that the company is meeting all state financial reporting requirements.

The third method to verify solvency is to require insurers to submit annual financial statements to state insurance departments in a prescribed format. The **National Association of Insurance Commissioners (NAIC)** has prescribed a format called the NAIC Annual Statement, which requires detailed information on premiums, expenses, investments, losses, **reserves**, and other financial information. These statements are analyzed to assess insurers' financial strength.

The fourth method to verify solvency is to administer the **Insurance Regulatory Information System (IRIS)**, which was also designed by the NAIC. IRIS helps regulators identify insurers with potential financial problems. It uses data from an insurer's financial statements to develop financial ratios that assess the insurer's overall financial condition. If the insurer has ratios that are outside predetermined norms, IRIS identifies the company for

---

Solvency surveillance
The process, conducted by state insurance regulators, of verifying the solvency of insurers and determining whether their financial condition enables them to meet their financial obligations and to remain in business.

National Association of Insurance Commissioners (NAIC)
An association of the commissioners of the insurance departments of each state, the District of Columbia, and the U.S. territories and possessions, whose purpose is to coordinate insurance regulation activities among the various state insurance departments.

Reserves
The amount the insurer estimates and sets aside to pay on an existing claim that has not been settled.

Insurance Regulatory Information System (IRIS)
An information and early-warning system established and operated by the NAIC to monitor the financial soundness of insurers.

regulatory attention. IRIS is meant to be an early warning system that might enable regulators to rehabilitate an insurer or, if rehabilitation is not practical, to minimize the losses from liquidation.

If the regulators determine an insurer is insolvent, the state insurance department places it in receivership. If the insurer cannot be rehabilitated, it is liquidated according to the state's insurance code. At that point the state's **guaranty fund** may be available to reduce the effects of the insurer insolvency. A guaranty fund cannot prevent insurer insolvency, but it does provide funds to pay unpaid claims of insolvent insurers licensed in a particular state.

Under a special provision in state insurer licensing laws, state regulators are empowered to partially or completely take over the operation of an insurer that has been determined to be in danger of failing to meet its financial obligations. In extreme cases, a state may even dissolve an insurer and assign administration of the existing policies to another insurer.

Guaranty fund
A state fund that provides a system to pay the claims of insolvent insurers, generally funded by assessments collected from all insurers licensed in the state.

SUMMARY

Insurers can be classified in these ways:

- Form of ownership, which includes stock insurance companies, mutual insurance companies, reciprocal insurance exchanges, Lloyds, captives, reinsurers, and government insurers
- Place of incorporation, which includes domestic, foreign, or alien
- Licensing status, which includes admitted insurers and nonadmitted insurers
- Common marketing systems used, which include independent agency and brokerage, exclusive agency, direct writer, and alternative distribution channels

Like many businesses, insurers pursue their goals by segmenting operations into functional areas, or departments. These departments must cooperate to serve the primary function of transferring the financial consequences of loss exposures and to meet other insurer goals. An insurer's key functions are marketing, underwriting, claims, loss control, and premium audit. Each department must interact effectively with other departments for the insurer to achieve its goals.

Insurers are regulated primarily for three reasons:

- To protect consumers
- To maintain insurer solvency
- To prevent destructive competition

All U.S. states have created an insurance department to regulate insurance sold in each state. The states focus their regulatory activity in five key areas:

- Licensing
- Insurance rates
- Insurance policies
- Market conduct
- Insurer solvency

Direct Your Learning

Underwriting Basics

Educational Objectives

After learning the content of this chapter and completing the corresponding course guide assignment, you should be able to:

- Identify the purpose of underwriting.
- Describe the major activities in the underwriting process.
- Explain how an insurer's underwriting results are measured using financial and nonfinancial tools.

Outline

Purpose of Underwriting

The Underwriting Process

Measuring Underwriting Results

Summary

Underwriting Basics

PURPOSE OF UNDERWRITING

Through its underwriting function, an insurer develops books of business and maintains profitability.

Insurance companies assume billions of dollars in financial risk annually, risk that is transferred to them from individuals and businesses via the insurance transaction. Insurance underwriters, using the underwriting process and various supporting underwriting tools, are employed by insurers to assess both their new and current business. An insurance company's overall profitability can depend significantly on the quality of its underwriting.

The purpose of underwriting is to help an insurance company develop and maintain a profitable book of business. For underwriting to achieve its purpose, insurers must control the effects of adverse selection and protect available **capacity**. For example, individuals and businesses owning property in an area prone to frequent coastal storms are generally very interested in buying property insurance that includes storm coverages such as wind, rain, hail, and flood. Insurance companies, however, usually do not want to provide property insurance to applicants who expect frequent, severe losses. Underwriters minimize the effects of adverse selection by carefully selecting the applicants whose loss exposures they are willing to insure.

Capacity
The amount of business an insurer is able to write, usually based on a comparison of the insurer's written premiums to its policyholders' surplus.

Adverse Selection—An Illustration

Insurers Most Willing to Provide Coverage for These Customers	
Customers With Lowest Probability of Loss	↔ Customer Likely to Purchase Insurance
Customers With Average Probability of Loss	↔ Customer More Likely to Purchase Insurance
Insurers Less Willing to Provide Coverage for These Customers	
Customers With Greatest Probability of Loss	↔ Customer Most Likely to Purchase Insurance

Written premium
The total premium on all policies written (put into effect) during a particular period.

An insurance company must have adequate policyholders' surplus if it wishes to increase its **written premium** volume. An insurer's capacity is limited by regulatory guidelines and often by its own voluntary constraints, which are frequently more conservative than those imposed by regulators. If an insurer's underwriting practices generate policy premiums that exceed losses and expenses, the policyholders surplus will increase, thereby increasing capacity.

THE UNDERWRITING PROCESS

Whether relying on independent judgment or the guidance of expert systems, underwriters engage in a series of activities designed to ensure that, ultimately, insurers are able to reach their business goals.

An underwriting decision regarding acceptability, in addition to other underwriting issues, must be made on every new insurance application submitted to an insurer. Underwriting decisions must also be made on renewal policies as well as on certain policy changes (such as a request to add a driver to an auto policy). Typically an insurance company **underwriter** makes these decisions. Underwriters increasingly use **expert systems**, which help them make better and more consistent underwriting decisions. Expert systems, also known as knowledge-based systems or rules-based systems, are most frequently used in personal lines and small commercial lines insurance, but their ability to handle large commercial accounts is growing.

Underwriter
An insurer employee who evaluates applicants for insurance, selects those that are acceptable to the insurer, prices coverage, and determines policy terms and conditions.

Expert systems
Computer software programs that supplement the underwriting decision-making process. These systems ask for the information necessary to make an underwriting decision, ensuring that no information is overlooked.

The underwriting process consists of these activities:

- Gathering the necessary information
- Making the underwriting decision
- Implementing the underwriting decision
- Monitoring the underwriting decision

Gathering the Necessary Information

To make a decision on new insurance accounts, as well as on certain renewal policies or policy changes, underwriters need adequate information to determine the potential risk each applicant represents. Underwriters can obtain information from the following sources:

- Producers—In addition to completing and submitting applications, producers might supply information not included on applications or renewals such as a business's annual report, a preliminary loss control review, or a producer's professional recommendation of an applicant.

- Consumer investigation reports—Several independent reporting services can investigate prospective insureds to obtain background information. Insurance applications generally inform applicants that they might be investigated.

- Government records—Motor vehicle records (MVRs) are commonly used in underwriting auto insurance. Underwriters can also seek pertinent information in court documents and public records relating to property ownership.
- Financial rating services—Firms such as Dun & Bradstreet (D&B) and Standard & Poor's (S&P) provide data on the credit rating and financial stability of specific businesses. In personal lines, some insurers use insurance scoring, a form of **predictive modeling** that uses a statistical analysis of credit report information to identify the relative likelihood of an insurance loss based on the actual loss experience of individuals with similar financial patterns.
- Inspection reports—Many insurance companies employ loss control representatives whose duties include physically inspecting the premises and reviewing the operations of insurance applicants and preparing reports for underwriters.
- Field marketing personnel—Insurers often have employees such as marketing representatives who spend much of their time in the field working with producers. These field personnel can often provide additional insights regarding an applicant based on visits to the prospective insured's premises in the company of a producer.
- Production records—In evaluating an application, an underwriter generally considers the history of the producer submitting it. If a producer has consistently generated profitable business, the underwriter might be willing to accept an applicant that does not meet all of the insurance company's underwriting standards.
- Premium audit reports—Rates for certain kinds of commercial insurance policies are applied to estimated payroll, sales, or some other exposure unit whose exact measure cannot be determined until the end of the policy year. Insurance companies employ premium auditors to obtain the final figures from insureds' accounting records in order to compute the final premiums on such policies. In addition, a premium auditor can often provide an underwriter with other information about an insured, especially if the auditor has visited the insured's premises and seen the insured's operations.
- Applicant's or insured's records—Underwriters can sometimes obtain information from an applicant's or insured's records, such as copies of jewelry appraisals (for valuation purposes) and property bills of sale. For businesses, the annual report, which describes a firm's operations and plans and contains its financial statements (including the balance sheet and income statement), provides much useful underwriting information. Most businesses have Web sites that also can be sources of valuable information.
- Claim files—An applicant's loss history is usually provided to an underwriter when an application is submitted to the insurance company. However, after a policy has been issued, an insured might file one or more

Predictive modeling
A process in which historical data based on behaviors and events are blended with multiple variables and used to construct models of anticipated future outcomes.

new claims. The claim process generates additional information which is then stored in, and accessible from, the insurance company's claim files.

Making the Underwriting Decision

After obtaining all pertinent information, an underwriter evaluates an application to determine the risk posed by the applicant, the underwriting options available, and the appropriate pricing.

One way an underwriter determines the level of risk posed by an applicant is by analyzing information about the conditions affecting the applicant, called hazards, that may increase the chance of loss. Examples of hazards are an inexperienced driver in regard to auto insurance and poor maintenance of fire extinguishers in regard to insurance on a building. To make an underwriting decision, an underwriter must consider whether the hazards presented by the applicant make the level of overall risk desirable or undesirable. In evaluating each application, an underwriter has three options:

- Accept the application without modification
- Reject the application
- Accept the application with modification

An application may be so desirable, or so undesirable, that the underwriter will accept it with no changes or reject it outright. The last option, accepting the application with modification, requires the greatest amount of underwriting expertise. Generally, the underwriter, producer, and applicant all want the insurance policy to be issued. If the particular coverage requested cannot be provided, the underwriter can often offer alternative terms and conditions that satisfy all parties. Alternatives available to underwriters to make a risk more acceptable include requiring additional loss control measures, modifying the policy provisions, and modifying the premium.

Often a policy can be issued if the applicant agrees to implement additional loss control measures. For example, an underwriter might agree to write property insurance for a particular bookstore provided the store owner installs and maintains an appropriate fire alarm system.

When a producer requests a particular set of policy provisions or insuring terms for an applicant, such as a coverage deductible or specific policy form, such provisions or terms are usually contingent upon an underwriter's review of the account. For example, if an applicant has an extensive loss history, the underwriter might recommend increasing the deductible, adding certain exclusions to the policy form requested, or using an alternative policy form that provides narrower coverage than the one requested. Each of these modifications reduces the insurer's exposure to loss.

Another possible way to make an application acceptable is to modify the price charged for the coverage. A producer might have quoted auto insurance using the insurer's "preferred risk" rate, which is a lower rate offered to substantially better-than-average applicants. The underwriter might determine that the applicant does not qualify as a preferred risk but would be acceptable for coverage at standard class prices.

After careful review of hazards, underwriting options, and pricing, the underwriter can then make the best possible decision available for a particular account. Each alternative presented, such as following loss control recommendations or accepting modified coverage, requires the agreement of the applicant and might involve further negotiation. In such situations, the underwriter normally contacts the producer to negotiate the issues with the applicant.

Implementing the Underwriting Decision

After making an underwriting decision, the underwriter implements the decision. All decisions, whether the application is accepted, rejected, or accepted with modification, are clearly communicated to the producer and to other insurance company personnel. If the underwriting decision is made using expert systems and the application is approved, the policy will automatically be issued to the producer and insured. This approach is typical with routine applications for auto insurance, homeowners insurance, and small commercial accounts. If the decision is not fully automated and is consistent with underwriting guidelines and within the underwriter's authority, the underwriter can approve the application for policy issuance.

Some applications an underwriter wants to approve may exceed the underwriter's authority and require a supervisor's approval. The supervisor might simply approve or reject the underwriter's recommendation or might refer the entire application to a more specialized or experienced underwriter for review. The second underwriter may approve, reject, or modify the first underwriter's recommendation.

Monitoring the Underwriting Decision

The underwriting process does not end when a policy is issued. The underwriter must continually monitor the results of the initial underwriting decision. Underwriters do this by monitoring claims activity on policies, monitoring the hazards that develop from changes to the policies, and monitoring the overall profitability of the book of business for which each underwriter is responsible.

By monitoring the nature and number of claims that develop, underwriters can evaluate whether additional underwriting action is required. The fact that an insured experiences a serious loss or several losses is not necessarily an indication that the underwriter made a bad decision. Conversely, a lack of serious losses does not necessarily mean that the underwriter made a good decision in accepting the account. The occurrence or the nonoccurrence of losses might be a matter of chance.

If serious problems develop with an account, the underwriter might need to take corrective action. Such action can include recommending additional loss control measures, modifying the terms of coverage, canceling coverage (if permitted by the regulatory authorities), or marking the policy for nonrenewal at the end of the current policy term.

During the policy term, the policyholder might request one or more coverage changes. The underwriter must carefully consider and implement each request as appropriate. Some changes present no increased hazard, while others might increase the potential for losses. For example, a change of vehicle on an automobile policy from a five-year-old sedan to a five-year-old coupe does not necessarily represent an increased hazard, but it might if at the same time a young driver is added as an additional operator.

Despite the variations in the hazards present or in the loss experience of individual accounts, the entire group of accounts handled by an underwriter is expected to meet the profitability goals established for the book of business. Careful monitoring of each account helps the underwriter meet these goals.

Finally, as the policy expiration date approaches, the underwriter might need to repeat the underwriting process before agreeing to renew the policy for another term. Renewal underwriting can generally be accomplished more quickly than new business underwriting because the insured is already known to the underwriter and more information might be available as claim reports or loss control reports have been added to the file. However, the underwriter must determine whether any changes in the account have occurred, and, if so, carefully go through the underwriting process again.

Many insurers do not repeat the entire underwriting process at every renewal for existing small commercial lines policies, such as businessowners policies (BOPs), or personal lines policies such as automobile and homeowners. Instead, they continue to renew these policies until a particular activity triggers an underwriting review. Claims, requests for coverage changes, or the passage of a certain amount of time might prompt an insurer to repeat the underwriting process.

The Underwriting Process
- Gathering the necessary information
- Making the underwriting decision
- Implementing the underwriting decision
- Monitoring the underwriting decision

MEASURING UNDERWRITING RESULTS

Insurers measure underwriting results using several financial and nonfinancial measures.

An insurer's underwriting results are a key indicator of its level of profitability. Without a clear understanding of underwriting performance, insurers may not be able to respond to conditions adversely affecting them or recognize opportunities to improve their performance. Insurance companies typically track their underwriting results through the use of financial measures and nonfinancial measures.

Financial Measures

Financial measures are calculations or ratios that describe a business's performance. These financial measures can be used to assess an insurance company's underwriting results:

- Loss ratio
- Expense ratio
- Combined ratio

The **loss ratio**, commonly expressed as a percentage, indicates what portion of the insurer's **earned premiums** goes to paying claims:

$$\text{Loss ratio} = \frac{\text{Incurred losses (including loss adjustment expenses)}}{\text{Earned premiums}} \times 100.$$

Loss ratio
The ratio of incurred losses and loss adjustment expenses to earned premiums.

Earned premiums
The portion of written premiums that corresponds to coverage that has already been provided.

By examining this percentage, an insurance company can assess how closely actual loss experience compares to expected loss experience. For example, at the beginning of the year, management might have decided that an 85 percent loss ratio is the coming year's target. The loss ratio is then continuously monitored by management to determine whether results meet expectations (that is, the loss ratio never exceeds 85 percent).

The **expense ratio**, commonly expressed as a percentage, indicates what portion of an insurer's written premiums is being used to pay the company's operating expenses, such as policy acquisition costs, general expenses, and premium taxes. In effect, this measures an insurance company's general cost of doing business as a proportion of the premiums it has written:

$$\text{Expense ratio} = \frac{\text{Underwriting expenses}}{\text{Written premiums}} \times 100.$$

Expense ratio
An insurer's incurred underwriting expenses for a given period divided by its written premiums for the same period.

The expense ratio provides an indication of how efficiently an insurance company is operating. Insurers monitor the expense ratio over time and attempt to

Combined ratio
The sum of an insurer's loss ratio and its expense ratio.

reduce it by managing the volume and pricing of policies written and controlling expenses.

The **combined ratio** is used to compare cash inflows and outflows from insurance operations. The combined ratio is calculated as follows:

$$\text{Combined ratio} = \text{Loss ratio} + \text{Expense ratio}.$$

From an insurer's perspective, the lower the combined ratio, the better. For example, a combined ratio of 95 percent means that an insurer has an outflow of $0.95 for every premium dollar, while a combined ratio of 115 percent means that the insurer has an outflow of $1.15 for every premium dollar. When the combined ratio is exactly 100 percent, every premium dollar is being used to pay claims and cover operating costs, with nothing remaining for insurer profit. When the combined ratio is greater than 100 percent, an **underwriting loss** occurs: more dollars are being paid out than are being taken in as premiums. When the combined ratio is less than 100 percent, an **underwriting profit** occurs because all premium dollars taken in are not being used for claims and expenses. Most insurers consider any combined ratio under 100 percent to be acceptable because it indicates a profit from underwriting results, even before income from an insurer's investment activity is considered in its overall financial performance.

Underwriting loss
An insurer's loss incurred when losses and expenses for a given period are greater than its premium earned for the same period.

Underwriting profit
Income an insurer earns from premiums paid by policyholders minus incurred losses and underwriting expenses.

Nonfinancial Measures

The success of an insurance company depends on the ability of every underwriter to attain and maintain profitable results over the long term. This profitability goal is accomplished, in part, through the use of nonfinancial measures to assess performance. Nonfinancial measures link an organization's business strategy and its outputs to its performance. In a general business context, two common examples of nonfinancial measures are the quality of customer service and the volume of goods produced. In the insurance industry, nonfinancial measures used to assess an insurer's underwriting results can include these:

- Product mix
- Pricing
- Retention ratio
- Success ratio
- Customer service

Some of these nonfinancial measures apply only to commercial lines underwriting departments, while others apply to both personal and commercial lines; portions of both types may be automated using expert systems. Some measures can be evaluated during an underwriting audit. Insurance company management and underwriting staff typically work together to agree on the nonfinancial measures, or standards, that comprise underwriting goals.

Product Mix

Measuring product mix is one way to evaluate an underwriter's contribution to a profitable book of business. Building a proper book of business requires that underwriters have a thorough knowledge of the insurer's business goals, including the types of products it prefers to write and the "appetite" the insurer has for certain types of risks. For example, one insurer may have a preference for writing automobile insurance in a particular state; while it also has the capacity to write homeowners insurance, it may prefer not to for business reasons. Another insurer, operating in the same state, could have exactly the opposite preferences. Underwriters working for each of these insurers would need to be aware of such preferences when considering new applicants. Underwriters are often held accountable for supporting product mix goals, provided the goals are clearly stated in company underwriting guidelines.

Pricing

Insurance companies generally set pricing standards as a nonfinancial measure. Pricing standards enable insurers to determine levels of premium adequacy by comparing premiums charged to the set pricing standards. For example, in commercial insurance, underwriters typically modify rates for each account being underwritten to reflect specific features of that account. Pricing standards indicate the extent to which these modifications depart from the insurer's regular or "standard" pricing. If one or more underwriters continually apply excessive premium credits to accounts in order to obtain new business or to retain it on renewal, an underwriting audit might reveal that profitability is being sacrificed in return for short-term growth.

Retention Ratio

The longer an insurance company retains a policy on its books, the more profitable (excluding claims activity) that account becomes. This is because of the expenses required to obtain and maintain an account during its first year with the company. Known as acquisition costs, these expenses include underwriting expenses, producer commissions, and loss control expenses, and they are often higher in a new policy term than in a renewal term. Too low a **retention ratio** might indicate serious deficiencies, such as poor service to producers, noncompetitive pricing, or unfavorable claim service. This nonfinancial measure requires careful monitoring of renewals, the competitive environment, and any industry trends that can affect retention.

Retention ratio
The percentage of insurance policies renewed.

Success Ratio

Increasingly, insurance company underwriters have dual responsibilities: they are not only responsible for underwriting their books of business; they are also known as "production underwriters," responsible for meeting any new business sales goals their employers make applicable to their books of business. Sometimes called the "hit ratio," a **success ratio** is a nonfinancial measure

Success ratio
The ratio of insurance policies written to those that have been quoted to applicants for insurance.

used to determine how well underwriters (or the company as a whole) are meeting their sales goals.

These factors can lead to a high success ratio:

- Competition is easing.
- Rates are inadequate or lower than other insurers' rates.
- Coverage is broader than other insurers' coverage.
- The underwriter has skill set for production underwriting.
- Underwriting selection criteria are relaxed.
- Service is excellent.

These factors can lead to a low success ratio:

- Competition is increasing.
- Rates are higher than other insurers' rates.
- Coverages or forms are too restrictive.
- The underwriter does not have skill set for production underwriting.
- Underwriting selection criteria are too strict.
- Service is poor.

Customer Service

Producers usually measure insurance company performance, in part, on the basis of customer service. An insurance company can also measure its service to producers (and direct service it provides to policyholders through service centers) by establishing a set of minimum acceptable standards for certain types of service. Examples of customer service standards include response time on issuing quotes, turnaround time on applications received, average number of errors per policy issued, response time on inquiries, and number of referrals for new business received. The actual performance of each underwriter, branch, or region being measured can be compared with the targeted level of performance.

Example of Measuring Customer Service

Category	Minimum Acceptable Standard
1. Quotations	Three working days
2. New policies	Three working days
3. Replies to correspondence	Two working days
4. Cancellations, endorsements, certificates	Five working days
5. Direct cancellation notices	Same-day service
6. Renewals	No later than ten days before expiration

SUMMARY

The purpose of underwriting is to help insurance companies develop and maintain a profitable book of business. Adverse selection and capacity inadequacies must be minimized for underwriting to achieve this purpose.

The underwriting process comprises a series of activities performed by underwriters, often with the assistance of expert systems, which help underwriters make better and more consistent decisions. The steps in the underwriting process include gathering the necessary information, making the underwriting decision, implementing the decision, and monitoring the decision.

An insurance company's underwriting results are a key indicator of its level of profitability. In order to measure the results of both individual and collective underwriting efforts, insurers use both financial measures and nonfinancial measures.

Direct Your Learning

CHAPTER 5

Claims Basics

Educational Objectives

After learning the content of this chapter and completing the corresponding course guide assignment, you should be able to:

▸ List the goals of the claim function.

▸ Identify the activities performed in the claim handling process and the purpose of each.

▸ Define the role of each of the following in the claim handling process:
- Claim managers
- Supervisors
- Claim representatives
- Technical specialists
- Customer service representatives
- Producers

▸ Explain how an insurer's claim results are measured using financial and nonfinancial tools.

Outline

Goals of the Claim Function

Activities in the Claim Handling Process

Roles of Claim Personnel

Measuring Claim Results

Summary

Claims Basics

GOALS OF THE CLAIM FUNCTION

The goals of the claim department include complying with the promise outlined in the policy by paying losses and supporting an insurer's profit goal.

People and organizations purchase property and casualty insurance policies to protect against financial losses that can result from property damage, bodily injury, or liability to others for losses for which these policyholders are legally responsible. When a policyholder or another party involved in a loss makes a claim against an insurance policy, the insurer is called upon to honor the promise made in the insurance contract, namely, to indemnify the policyholder for financial losses. This does not imply that the insurer should or will pay every claim that is presented; rather, it implies that the insurer's claim department will conduct a good-faith investigation of a claim and pay only legitimate claims for causes of loss that are insured by the policy.

An insurance organization's senior management establishes the goals for the claim function. In establishing these goals, managers must equally consider the needs of the insurance customer (the policyholder) and the needs of the insurer. The claim function typically has two primary goals:

- Compliance with the contractual promise
- Support of the insurer's profit goal

Compliance With the Contractual Promise

The first goal of the claim function is to satisfy the insurer's obligations to the policyholder as set forth in the insurance contract. Following a loss, the insurer seeks to fulfill the promise set out in the insuring agreement to pay, defend, or indemnify the insured in the event of a covered loss.

The insurer fulfills this promise by providing fair, prompt, and equitable service to the policyholder either directly, when the loss involves a **first-party claim** made by the policyholder against the insurer, or indirectly, when the loss involves a **third-party claim** made against the policyholder by someone to whom the policyholder may be liable.

> **First-party claim**
> A demand by an insured person or organization seeking to recover from its insurer for a loss that its insurance policy may cover.
>
> **Third-party claim**
> A demand by a third party against an insured based on the legal duties the insured owes to the third party; it seeks to recover from the insured's insurer for a loss that the issuing policy may cover.

> **Parties to the Insurance Contract**
>
> Insurance coverage is often referred to as either first-party insurance or third-party insurance.
>
> Property insurance is considered first-party insurance because the insurer makes payment for covered losses directly to the insured. Liability insurance is considered third-party insurance because the insurer makes payments on behalf of the insured (first party) to a claimant (third party) who is injured or whose property is damaged by the insured.

Claimant
Anyone who submits a claim to an insurer.

Claim representative
The person responsible for investigating, evaluating, and settling claims.

The insurance contract is marketed not only as a financial mechanism to restore policyholders and other **claimants** to a pre-loss state, but also as a way for policyholders to achieve peace of mind. For a claimant, a loss occurrence and the consequences are not routine and can be overwhelming. A **claim representative** should handle claims in a way that promotes peace of mind for the policyholder who has suffered a loss and that quickly restores a claimant to his or her pre-loss condition.

Support of the Insurer's Profit Goal

The second goal of the claim function is to support the insurer's profit goal. Achieving this goal is generally the responsibility of the marketing and underwriting departments; however, the claim function serves a role in generating underwriting profit by controlling expenses and paying only legitimate claims.

By managing all claim function expenses, setting appropriate spending policies, and using appropriately priced providers and services, claim managers can help maintain an insurer's underwriting profit. Similarly, claim staff can avoid overspending on costs of handling claims, claim operations, or other expenses. Finally, by ensuring fair claim settlement, claim representatives prevent any unnecessary increase in the cost of insurance and subsequent reduction in the insurer's underwriting profit.

Policyholders and other claimants are likely to accept an insurer's settlement offer if they believe they are receiving fair treatment. Parties who believe they have been treated unfairly may seek to settle their differences with the insurer by filing lawsuits. Litigation erodes goodwill between the parties and generates increased claim expenses, reducing the insurer's profitability. Additionally, dissatisfied policyholders or claimants may complain to their state insurance department and, if the state regulatory authorities find fault, an insurer may be subjected to regulatory oversight or penalties. Costs associated with regulatory action can further erode an insurer's profits.

An insurer's success in achieving its profit goal is reflected in its reputation for providing the service promised. A reputation for resisting legitimate claims can undermine the effectiveness of an insurer's advertising. Consequently, the two goals of the claim function work together for a profitable insurance operation.

ACTIVITIES IN THE CLAIM HANDLING PROCESS

The activities in the claim handling process provide a guideline for effectively handling all types of claims regardless of the severity or complexity of the loss.

Claim handling is the insurer function that processes demands for claim payments. Different insurers use different names to describe claim handling, and some terms are used in specific instances; for example, in property claims, the term "loss adjusting" is often used instead of claim handling. Terms may include claim adjusting, loss adjusting, claim processing, and claim examining; but all refer to the same claim function: complying with the contractual promise made in the insurance policy to satisfy the insurer's obligation to the policyholder.

Claim handling
The insurer function that processes demands for claim payments.

The claim handling process is made up of six activities:

1. Acknowledging a claim and assigning it to a claim representative
2. Identifying the policy
3. Contacting the insured or the insured's representative
4. Investigating and documenting the claim
5. Determining cause of loss and loss amount
6. Concluding the claim

These activities are not sequential, but instead can begin and end at any point in the process and can overlap. Depending on the severity and complexity of the loss, claim handling can be a quick process, completed within hours or days after submission of a claim report, or it can extend over many months or even years.

Acknowledging a Claim and Assigning It to a Claim Representative

The first claim handling activity the insurer performs is acknowledging receipt of the claim and assigning it to a claim representative. When a loss occurs, the policyholder or the insured reports the loss to the producer, who submits it to the insurer, or the policyholder or insured may report the loss directly to the insurer. In many instances, the policyholder and insured are the same, but not in every instance.

The insurer acknowledges receipt of the claim by taking the loss information and creating a claim file. A claim representative is assigned to handle the loss. The claim representative may be a member of the insurer's claim department staff, such as a telephone or field claim representative, or may work for an independent adjusting firm (a business that contracts with insurers to handle claims).

ACORD Property Loss Notice

ACORD PROPERTY LOSS NOTICE

DATE (MM/DD/YYYY): 8/1/0X

PRODUCER	PHONE (A/C, No, Ext): INS AGENCY TEL # 3
PAUL PROCTOR	
PLAINFIELD, OH	
CODE: 39542	SUB CODE:
AGENCY CUSTOMER ID	

MISCELLANEOUS INFO (Site & location code): 215 555-2100
DATE OF LOSS AND TIME: 7/29/0X [X] AM [ ] PM
PREVIOUSLY REPORTED: YES [X] NO [ ]

POLICY TYPE	COMPANY AND POLICY NUMBER	NAIC CODE	POLICY DATES
PROP/HOME	CO: IIA / POL: HO 1894370	39542	EFF: 6/16/0X EXP: 6/16/0Y
FLOOD	CO: / POL:		EFF: / EXP:
WIND	CO: / POL:		EFF: / EXP:

INSURED / CONTACT

NAME AND ADDRESS OF INSURED
LEONARD HILLMAN
156 SIXTH AVENUE
PLAINFIELD, OH 48740

RESIDENCE PHONE (A/C, No): 215 555-8181
BUSINESS PHONE (A/C, No, Ext): 215 555-5000

NAME AND ADDRESS OF SPOUSE (IF APPLICABLE):

CONTACT — CONTACT INSURED
NAME AND ADDRESS OF INSURED: JULIA HILLMAN
RESIDENCE PHONE: 215 555-8181
WHERE TO CONTACT: HOME
WHEN TO CONTACT: ANYTIME

LOSS

LOCATION OF LOSS:
POLICE OR FIRE DEPT TO WHICH REPORTED:

KIND OF LOSS: FIRE [ ] LIGHTNING [ ] FLOOD [ ] OTHER (explain) [ ]
THEFT [ ] HAIL [X] WIND [X]

PROBABLE AMOUNT ENTIRE LOSS: $5,000

DESCRIPTION OF LOSS & DAMAGE: WIND AND HAIL SERIOUSLY DAMAGED ROOF AND BLEW SHINGLES OFF. CONTENTS INSIDE ALSO DAMAGED.

POLICY INFORMATION

MORTGAGEE: PLAINFIELD FEDERAL SAVINGS AND LOAN ASSOCIATION
[ ] NO MORTGAGEE

HOMEOWNER POLICIES SECTION 1 ONLY (Complete for coverages A, B, C, D & additional coverages. For Homeowners Section II Liability Losses, use ACORD 3.)

A. DWELLING	B. OTHER STRUCTURES	C. PERSONAL PROPERTY	D. LOSS OF USE	DEDUCTIBLES	DESCRIBE ADDITIONAL COVERAGES PROVIDED
$90,000	$9,000	$45,000	$18,000	$100	

[ ] COVERAGE A. EXCLUDES WIND
SUBJECT TO FORMS: HO-3 INFLATION GUARD

FIRE, ALLIED LINES & MULTI-PERIL POLICIES (Complete only those items involved in loss)

ITEM	SUBJECT OF INSURANCE	AMOUNT	% COINS	DEDUCTIBLE	COVERAGE AND/OR DESCRIPTION OF PROPERTY INSURED
	[ ] BLDG [ ] CNTS				
	[ ] BLDG [ ] CNTS				
	[ ] BLDG [ ] CNTS				

SUBJECT TO FORMS:

FLOOD POLICY	BUILDING:	DEDUCTIBLE:	ZONE	PRE FIRM / POST FIRM	DIFF IN ELEV	FORM TYPE	GENERAL / DWELLING	CONDO
	CONTENTS:	DEDUCTIBLE:						

WIND POLICY	BUILDING	DEDUCTIBLE	CONTENTS	ZONE	FORM TYPE	GENERAL / DWELLING	CONDO

REMARKS/OTHER INSURANCE: NO OTHER INSURANCE.

CAT #	FICO #	ADJUSTER ASSIGNED		ADJUSTER #	DATE ASSIGNED

REPORTED BY: LEONARD HILLMAN
REPORTED TO: ANN ADAMS
SIGNATURE OF INSURED:
SIGNATURE OF PRODUCER: *Paul Proctor*

ACORD 1 (2002/01) — NOTE: IMPORTANT STATE INFORMATION ON REVERSE SIDE — © ACORD CORPORATION 1988

© ACORD. Used with permission.

Identifying the Policy

The claim representative identifies the insurance policy under which the claim is filed and checks it to determine whether it applies to the loss, the coverages that might apply, and the amount of coverage. In addition, the claim representative usually establishes **loss reserves**. However, some claims are concluded immediately without establishing reserves.

In some cases, reserves are established as "record only," when the insured wants the insurer to have a record of the incident but is not making a claim under the policy. For example, the insured auto is struck by another vehicle and sustains minor damage. The insured wishes to pursue collecting damages directly from the insurer of the car that struck his auto. The insured reports the accident to his own insurer as a record-only claim in order to preserve his right to pursue the claim with his insurer should his efforts to collect from the other driver's insurer fail. Some insurers will set up a minimum reserve on record-only files; others will not.

Loss reserves
Estimates of the amount of money the insurer expects to pay in the future for losses that have already occurred and been reported.

Contacting the Insured or the Insured's Representative

In most cases, the claim representative contacts the insured or the insured's representative soon after establishing reserves. The claim representative may schedule a time to meet with the insured or a party representing the insured at the loss location as part of the initial contact and verification of coverage.

Investigating and Documenting the Claim

Investigating and documenting the claim are ongoing activities the claim representative performs to create a complete **claim file**. Claim representatives commonly conduct many investigations, such as insured/witness investigations, claimant investigations, accident scene investigations, and medical investigations. They may consult numerous experts as a part of these investigations.

Claim file
A paper or an electronic file that contains information for a loss.

Experts Consulted in Claims

Experts Consulted in Property Claims	Experts Consulted in Liability Claims
• Origin and cause experts	• Accident reconstruction specialists
• Private investigators	• Accountants
• Accountants	• Lawyers
• Restoration specialists	• Private investigators
• Salvors	• Medical experts
• Lawyers	• SIUs
• Professionals needed to rebuild	
• Appraisers	
• Special investigation units (SIUs)	

Subrogation
The process by which an insurer can, after it has paid a loss under the policy, recover the amount paid from any party (other than the insured) who caused the loss or is otherwise legally liable for the loss.

In conjunction with their investigations, claim representatives also investigate **subrogation** possibilities to determine whether the insurer can recover any payments it has made from a third party that is legally responsible for the loss.

Claim representatives document claims based on the type of loss. For example, in addition to the file status notes, a medical liability claim might include recorded statements of witnesses, copies of medical bills, a physician's diagnosis, and a diagram of the accident scene; in contrast, a broken windshield claim might include only an estimate for the glass replacement with the claim representative's file status notes. Many insurers have claim handling guidelines for documenting each type of claim. Documenting a claim can involve these activities:

- Gathering records
- Photographing or taking visual recordings of a loss scene
- Drawing diagrams of damaged areas or accident scenes
- Reviewing the loss notice and financial records or examining inventory to determine the scope of loss
- Taking statements of the involved parties and witnesses
- Obtaining medical records

Determining Cause of Loss and Loss Amount

The claim representative then uses the results of the investigations and the claim documentation as a basis for determining the cause of loss and loss amount. The claim representative compares the information from the loss investigation to the terms of the policy to determine whether the policy covers the cause of loss. If so, the claim representative determines the amount of the loss, in terms of **property damage**, **bodily injury**, or **personal injury**.

Property damage
Physical injury to, destruction of, or loss of use of tangible property.

Bodily injury
Physical injury to a person, including sickness, disease, and death.

Personal injury
Injury, other than bodily injury, arising from intentional torts such as libel, slander, or invasion of privacy.

Concluding the Claim

Once the cause of loss and the loss amount are determined, the claim can be concluded. The claim representative prepares a loss statement and proceeds to settle the claim. Covered claims are settled with the policyholder or claimant or their representative through negotiation or alternative means of resolution, and the claim representative issues appropriate payments. Claims not covered by the policy are denied. Finally, the claim representative completes closing reports to properly document the claim. These reports enable insurers to track loss payments and claim handling practices, and they complete the documentation if a claim is later litigated.

Claims Basics 5.9

Example of a Scope Sheet

Property Loss Worksheet

Page No. ___1___
Preliminary Estimate ___10/19/XX___
Date

Final Estimate _____ ___M. Boyer___
Date   Claim Representative

Claim No. ___524 BL 101___
Insured ___J. Smith___
Claimant ___Insured___

1 Item	2 Description	3 Quantity	4 Units / Age	5 Unit price / Orig. cost	6 Cost / Repl. cost	7 Deprec.	8 A.C.V.	9 Loss & Damage
1.	Permit (if required)							

2.	Demolition
	  Remove range hood
	  Remove cabinets (4 LF)
	  Remove drywall
	  (above cabinet)
	  (5' x 10' = 50 SF)
	  Remove Formica countertop (12 LF)
	  (est. 2 men x 5 hrs. = 10 hrs.)							

3.	Cartage 1 pickup & driver (1.5 hrs.) Dump fee ($10.00)							
4.	Clean range (est. 1.5 hrs.)							
5.	Install new range hood (Lowe's 30", est. 1 hr.)							

6.	Install upper cabinets
	  Paint grade plywood of 4 LF x 3' tall
	  (est. 1.5 hrs.)							

7.	New Formica countertop							
8.	Drywall (above range) 5' × 10' = 50 sq. ft. Tape and texture (splatter finish)							
9.	Painting Kitchen—wash and paint (14' x 8') x 2 = 224 SF (20' x 8') x 2 = 320 SF 1 coat high-gloss latex 2 coats on new cabinets Living Room—wash and paint 1 coat flat latex (20' x 8') x 2 = 320SF (24' x 8') x 2 = 384 SF Entrance Hall (4' x 8') = 32 SF (14' x 8') x 2 = 224 SF							
10.	Shampoo carpets LR and halls (200 sq. yds.)							
11.	Clean vinyl tile in kitchen (280 SF)							
12.	Clean furniture (per estimate)							
13.	Contractor overhead & profit (OH/P 15% or 20%)							

ROLES OF CLAIM PERSONNEL

Claim personnel have many roles in effectively performing the claim handling process.

Insured
Any person or organization who is insured under an insurance policy.

Insurers, producers, and independent adjusting firms and other claim organizations employ claim personnel to fulfill the contractual promise that insurers make to their **insureds** in insurance policies. Claim department structures and job titles used to describe claim personnel vary among the different types of organizations; however, claim personnel perform basically the same roles despite these differences. The various roles of claim personnel are discussed here using common job titles:

- Claim managers
- Supervisors
- Claim representatives
- Technical specialists
- Customer service representatives
- Producers

Claim Managers

A claim manager directs and supervises the activities of some portion of an insurer's claim department. A claim department may have multiple levels of claim managers. An insurer's management team may include a claim vice president who supervises one or more assistant vice presidents. Assistant vice presidents may be assigned to specific types of insurance, such as workers compensation or auto insurance. Managers at the middle-management level, who may report to assistant vice presidents, usually have the title of claim manager.

A producer organization may have multiple levels of claim managers or none, depending on the volume of business the producer handles. A small firm may have a single general manager who also supervises the producer's claim function.

Some claim departments are divided into sub-departments, each with its own manager. For example, separate managers might oversee property losses, liability losses, workers compensation losses, subrogation, fraud investigation, appraisal, and legal work. Each claim manager may have these responsibilities that affect the claim process:

- Setting goals
- Developing staff members' skills
- Monitoring workloads
- Monitoring losses and expenses
- Establishing claim procedures and ensuring compliance

Managers set department goals related to claim handling, such as concluding claims that are ready for settlement, managing the cost of each claim, and recovering subrogation amounts.

Managers encourage employees to develop their professional skills through training in areas such as improved decision-making, claim handling efficiency, and other insurance-related topics. Such training may be offered in-house, through outside courses, or through online courses or software provided by training vendors. Managers may also encourage their employees to seek independent learning opportunities or to work toward professional insurance designations.

Managers monitor workloads to ensure that each claim representative is assigned a manageable number of claim files. Appropriate workload can be determined by the claim representative's experience, expertise, and time-management skills; the type of claim; and any procedures for documentation, reporting, and on-site inspections. Keeping workloads manageable also entails ensuring that employees have the resources required to work efficiently.

Managers also monitor losses and expenses to identify trends that may indicate the need for additional or specialized training, improvements in claim-handling practices, or additional staff.

Finally, claim managers establish procedures to ensure that claims are handled promptly and efficiently, in compliance with the organization's guidelines and with state insurance regulations.

Supervisors

Claim supervisors support the claim management functions of the managers to whom they report. In some organizations, claim departments are divided into units by line of business, such as auto or property, or by geographic location, such as state or designated territories. Each unit has a supervisor who directs its daily activities. Below the supervisor level, reporting relationships vary greatly depending on the structure of the organization.

Supervisors periodically monitor claim files to ensure consistent and accurate claim handling. Claim file reviews help supervisors evaluate claim representatives' performance, develop strategies for solving problems, and determine staff training needs. A supervisor might review each claim file, select only those files that meet specific criteria (such as those with reserves that exceed a certain amount), or examine a random sample of files. Some organizations employ quality control staff to review claim files rather than assign the duty to supervisors.

Claim supervisors usually have technical expertise and often train claim representatives who report to them; for example, they may use informal training meetings to update staff on medical and legal developments that affect claims or on other claim issues. They may also encourage staff members to pursue continuing professional education.

Claim Representatives

Organizations may employ different types of claim representatives, including telephone claim representatives, field claim representatives, and specialized claim representatives.

Telephone Claim Representatives

Telephone claim representatives, or **inside claim representatives**, handle claims from the organization's office. They investigate claims and evaluate **damages** based on telephone interviews and correspondence. If additional information or expertise is needed to thoroughly investigate a loss, they may ask field claim representatives for assistance. Telephone claim representatives can handle small, uncomplicated claims or larger, more complex claims, as determined by claim department procedures and the types of insurance policies the insurer writes. For example, telephone claim representatives may handle personal auto claims or bodily injury claims, and they might review damage estimates to settle certain property losses. Some organizations use telephone claim representatives to handle nearly every claim.

Field Claim Representatives

Claim representatives who work both inside and outside the organization's office are called **field claim representatives**, or **outside claim representatives**. They generally handle claims that require investigating the scene of a loss; resolving complex investigative issues; or meeting with insureds, claimants, lawyers, and others involved in the claim. Field claim representatives inspect damaged property and work closely with damage appraisers. They often prepare damage estimates, obtain photos and diagrams of accident locations, and negotiate settlements with claimants or their representatives.

An insurer's claim staff may not always be sufficient to complete its claim handling activities. In such cases, additional claim representatives are available through independent adjusting firms. An insurer may contract with these firms when it needs expertise in handling a specific type of claim, when losses have occurred in an area where the insurer has no assigned claim representatives, or when the insurer's claim staff is insufficient to handle current caseloads.

Specialized Claim Representatives

Depending on the size of a claim organization, claim representatives may specialize in a particular type of claim. The increasing complexities in the claim handling environment often require such specialization. A claim representative who specializes by line of business or state can focus on developing expertise only in the laws and regulations relating to the specialty or state, rather than developing a broader range of knowledge.

Telephone claim representative, or **inside claim representative**
An insurer employee who handles claims that can be settled by phone, mail, or e-mail from inside the insurer's office.

Damages
Money claimed by, or a monetary award to, a party who has suffered bodily injury or property damage for which another party is legally responsible.

Field claim representative, or **outside claim representative**
An insurer employee who handles claims that cannot be handled easily by phone, mail, or e-mail.

Claim representatives may specialize in these areas:

- Auto physical damage
- Building physical damage
- Heavy equipment damage
- Maritime property damage
- Automobile liability
- Workers compensation
- Homeowners liability
- General liability

For example, a damage appraiser is a field claim representative that specializes in auto physical damage appraisals. An insured with a damaged, but still drivable, auto can take it to a drive-in claim center, where a damage appraiser estimates the cost to repair the vehicle. Damage appraisers prepare their estimates using computer software or **crash manuals**, which may be automated. Based on the estimate, the damage appraiser may immediately issue a check to the insured. The insured can then choose where to have the car repaired. Alternatively, the insured may give the appraiser a damage estimate from a repair facility, and if the appraiser agrees with the estimate, he or she issues the insured a check for the estimate amount.

Crash manual
A book that describes procedures for estimating the cost to repair damage to vehicles and that lists auto part prices and typical labor times to repair or replace the part.

Field claim representatives may also specialize in heavy construction or pollution liability claims. Because of their expertise, these specialists can often suggest ways to reduce damage amounts. For example, a pollution liability specialist might know whom to contact to quickly contain a pollutant spill and reduce the resulting damage.

Some claim representatives specialize in handling catastrophe claims. Catastrophe claim specialists are trained to handle disasters (such as floods, hurricanes, tornadoes, and earthquakes) that result in multiple losses. Catastrophe claim specialists may travel to the site of a catastrophe, such as a hurricane, and remain there until all claims have been investigated.

Technical Specialists

Technical specialists assist insurers in determining liability and damages relating to claims. For example, they can help determine who is at fault in an accident, and thus, whether a claim should be paid. Technical specialists may work for a claim organization, such as an independent adjusting firm or a **third-party administrator**, or for a vendor that provides related services. Technical specialists include these:

- Origin and cause experts
- Material damage appraisers
- Reconstruction experts
- Medical consultants
- Rehabilitation nurses

Third-party administrator
An organization that provides administrative services associated with risk financing and insurance.

Total loss
A loss that exists when the cost to repair a damaged vehicle (or other property) equals or exceeds the value of the vehicle.

Constructive total loss
A loss such that property cannot be repaired for less than its actual cash value minus the anticipated salvage value.

Actual cash value
Cost to replace property with new property of like kind and quality less depreciation.

Salvage
The process by which an insurer takes possession of damaged property for which it has paid a total loss and recovers a portion of the loss payment by selling the damaged property.

Origin and cause experts investigate fire losses to determine where and how a fire began. Claim personnel often consult these specialists for fires of suspicious origin or when they believe that subrogation possibilities exist. Origin and cause experts use their background in fire science and arson investigation to determine whether a fire started accidentally or was set deliberately. They investigate fire scenes, contact witnesses, and seek the assistance of private investigators and engineers when needed.

Material damage appraisers inspect damage to autos and other types of property to determine whether the property is repairable, a **total loss**, or a **constructive total loss**. A vehicle is a total loss when the cost to repair it equals or exceeds its value. A vehicle is a constructive total loss when it cannot be repaired for less than its **actual cash value (ACV)** minus the anticipated salvage value. **Salvage** is damaged property the insurer can sell to recover part of the claim payment. Generally, material damage appraisers help determine damages only and not coverage and liability. If the property can be repaired, they estimate the repair costs and negotiate the repair price with the insured's selected repair facility, contractor, body shop, or other organization. If the property is a total loss, the appraiser helps the claim representative determine the value of the property and helps locate a buyer for any salvage.

Reconstruction experts specialize in reconstructing the events surrounding automobile accidents. They can describe how an accident occurred and can provide legal testimony as to the vehicles' speeds, braking distances, and what the drivers involved could see before the impact.

Medical consultants and rehabilitation nurses are technical specialists that help claim personnel assess the medical requirements in injury claims. Medical consultants arrange independent medical examinations (IMEs), called defense medical exams (DMEs) in some jurisdictions, for injured insureds and claimants and request second opinions from physicians for treatments or surgical procedures. Medical consultants also review medical reports and audit bills from physicians and other medical providers to determine whether the treatment being provided follows the physician's treatment instructions. Rehabilitation nurses help claim representatives assess whether or to what extent rehabilitation is possible for a claimant. In the field of medical consulting, specialized computer software offers another technical resource for handling claims. For example, medical evaluation software uses artificial intelligence to help claim representatives analyze appropriate medical services.

Customer Service Representatives

The customer service representative (CSR) is often the insured's or claimant's first contact with the insurer and with the claim handling process. When an insured or a claimant reports a loss directly to the insurer, a CSR generally records the loss information. Some CSRs have limited authority to handle routine claims, such as windshield damage claims. CSRs also answer telephone inquiries and perform routine processing and clerical tasks.

Claims Basics 5.15

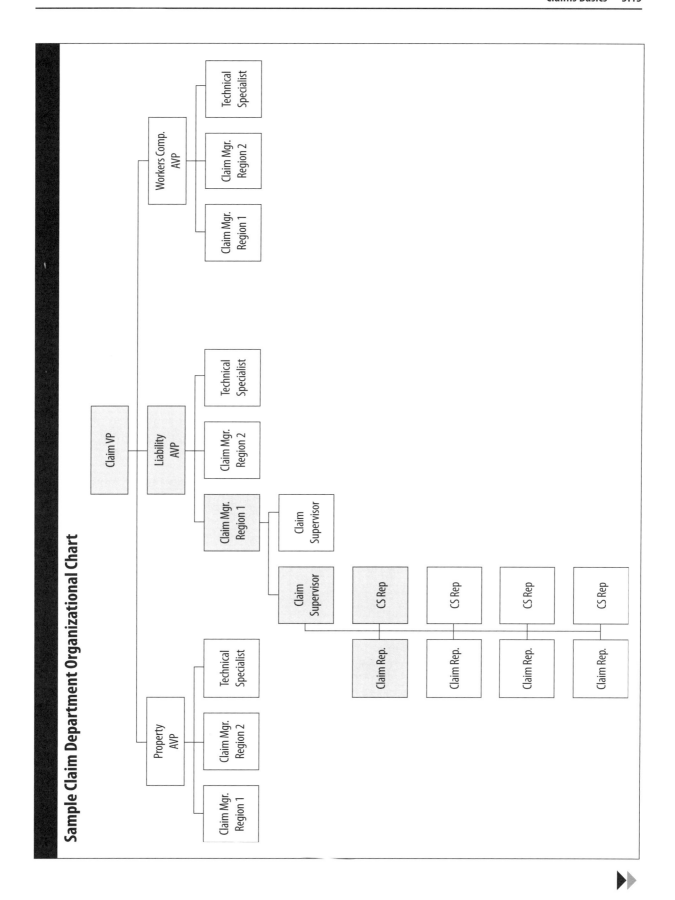

Producers

Insurance producers are often involved in the claim handling process. Some insureds call their producer first when a loss occurs. Producers record these claims and may assist the insured in the claim process. Providing this service, beyond their primary role of locating insurance coverage, gives producers an opportunity to demonstrate their value to their customers.

Most insurers who market insurance through independent agents give **draft authority** to selected **agents** within a producer organization to settle certain types of claims up to a specified amount, such as $2,500. Generally, agents can use draft authority only to handle claims that require no liability determination, such as property damage to a home or automobile caused by an insured. Authorized agents can issue drafts (checks) directly to insureds for covered claims. In this capacity, producers perform a role similar to that of a telephone claim representative, but only for small claims. If none of a producer's agents have draft authority, the producer immediately reports the loss to the insurer, gives the insured the telephone number of the insurer's claim office, and explains how the insured can expect the claim to be handled.

Draft authority
The authority expressly given to an agent by an insurer allowing the agent to settle and pay certain types of claims up to a specified limit.

Agent
In the agency relationship, the party that is authorized by the principal to act on the principal's behalf.

MEASURING CLAIM RESULTS

Claim results can be determined through claim performance measures, internal standards by which the claim function and individual adjusters can be evaluated.

Insurers are businesses; business managers are responsible for organizations' profitability. Managers in most insurance organizations develop goals for the organization, their departments, and individual staff members to ensure the organization's profit. The efficiency with which employees perform their jobs can affect an organization's profitability. An insurer's claim results, achieved by accomplishing the goals of the claim function, are a crucial factor in determining overall profitability.

When the claim department pays fair amounts for legitimate claims and provides accurate, reliable, and consistent ratemaking data, the insurer's profitability goals are advanced. Conversely, poor claim results can undermine otherwise advantageous underwriting and marketing results.

Claim results are based on the insurer's profitability and the quality of its business practices. Two types of performance measures are used to evaluate an insurer's claim function: financial measures and nonfinancial measures.

Financial Measures

Managers periodically use various financial measures to evaluate claim results based on the insurer's solvency using predefined performance objectives, including the insurer's loss ratio, the combined ratio, and reserving accuracy.

An insurer's loss ratio is a financial measure that evaluates the insurer's financial solvency, and therefore its ability to meet its claim payment obligations. Consequently, the loss ratio is a measure of claim results. The loss ratio is developed from other figures: **incurred losses**, **loss adjustment expenses (LAE)**, and earned premiums.

The loss ratio can indicate one of three states of an insurer's financial condition: increasing, decreasing, or stable. An increasing loss ratio can be a sign of the insurer's pending financial difficulties; a decreasing loss ratio can indicate that the insurer is becoming more profitable; and a stable loss ratio can indicate that the insurer's profitability is unchanged. An increasing loss ratio can result from one or more factors. For example, the claim function could be operating inefficiently, underwriting could be selecting below-average loss exposures, or the actuarial department's pricing of the insurer's products may be inaccurate.

Managers use the loss ratio in calculating the insurer's combined ratio, another financial measure used to evaluate claim results. The loss ratio is added to the insurer's expense ratio to determine the combined ratio. The expense ratio compares the insurer's **underwriting expenses** with its written premiums for a given period.

Determining the accuracy with which loss reserves are set provides another financial measure to evaluate claim results. Claim staff set loss reserves when a claim is presented. Claim representatives monitor and adjust these reserves throughout the claim handling process to ensure that they continue to represent the approximate amount the insurer will pay for existing claims. Reserves should provide managers with a good estimation of the insurer's liability for existing claims to ensure accuracy of the insurer's financial reporting. To satisfy state insurance regulations, insurers must allocate funds on their **balance sheets** to cover reserve totals. If reserves are inadequate, the insurer must transfer sums from its policyholders' surplus to pay claims. Inadequate reserving creates a false impression of the insurer's financial worth as reflected on its financial statements.

Nonfinancial Measures

Nonfinancial measures can also be used to evaluate claim results. Managers use nonfinancial measures to evaluate the effectiveness of the claim function and the performance of individual claim representatives. Nonfinancial measures commonly include best practices, other nonfinancial criteria, claim audits, and customer feedback.

In a claim department, best practices usually refer to a system of identified individual practices that produce superior performance. Best practices are usually documented and shared with all claim managers and claim representatives. Claim managers can identify best practices by examining their own performance and by reviewing unfair claim practices acts. Claim department best practices may also be based on other legal requirements specified by

Incurred losses
The losses that have occurred during a specific period, no matter when claims resulting from the losses are paid.

Loss adjustment expenses (LAE)
Expenses that an insurer incurs to investigate, defend, and settle claims.

Underwriting expenses
Costs incurred by an insurer for operations, taxes, fees, and the acquisition of new policies.

Balance sheet
The financial statement that reports the assets, liabilities, and owners' equity of an organization as of a specific date.

> **Balancing and Controlling Loss Adjustment Expenses**
>
> Good claim handling practices should not be sacrificed in order to reduce loss adjustment expenses. For example, paying demanded settlements without properly investigating claims would reduce the expenses of investigation; however, in the long term, it would result in greater settlement amounts, which would increase the loss ratio.
>
> An insurer's claim handling guidelines provide claim handling policies and procedures that are designed to result in fair and effective claim settlement while minimizing expenses. Good-faith claim handling—considering the interests of the insured as much as the interests of the insurer—also helps control expenses by minimizing lawsuits and bad-faith claims against the insurer.

regulators, legislators, and the courts. Best practices for claim departments address matters such as these:

- Timely claim acknowledgement
- Timely response to outside communications
- Timely and accurate loss reserving
- Timely payment of claims or timely denial of claims
- Complete explanation of payments or denials
- File documentation standards

Other nonfinancial criteria for evaluating the claim function include these:

- Claim turnover—the average time it takes for open claims to be closed
- Number and percentage of litigated claims
- Ratio of successfully litigated claims to unsuccessfully litigated claims
- Average caseload per claim representative—the average number of claims each claim representative has open at any time
- Staff turnover—overall frequency of staff member changes resulting from retirements, other employment opportunities, and disciplinary actions

Other nonfinancial criteria for evaluating individual claim representatives' performance include these:

- File turnover—the time it takes a claim representative to handle a claim
- Ratio of litigated claims to nonlitigated claims
- Comparison of average settlement costs among claim representatives who handle similar claims

Claim audits can ensure compliance with best practices and can be used to gather statistical claim information using other nonfinancial criteria. Those who audit claims review a number of open and closed claim files, evaluating both qualitative and quantitative factors. Data derived from claim audits give insurance managers a snapshot of how well a claim department and individual claim representatives perform the claim function and, consequently, the overall effectiveness of the claim function. Specific measures can reveal flaws in the claim handling process and identify areas where the department or individual claim representatives require further training or education.

Customer feedback and survey results often suggest ways in which the claim function can improve the customer experience and better serve its policyholders. Customer feedback can come from many sources, such as directly from an insured, a claimant, or a vendor; or indirectly from a state insurance department on behalf of an insured, claimant, or vendor. Claim management must investigate complaints submitted to a state insurance department and respond to them in a timely manner.

SUMMARY

The two primary goals of the claim function are compliance with the contractual promise and support of the insurer's profit goal. Claim personnel help meet these goals by using the claim handling process to promptly, fairly, and equitably pay all legitimate first- and third-party claims and by managing operational and claim handling expenses. Policyholders' satisfaction that the insurer's contractual promises have been met promotes goodwill and supports an insurer's profit goals.

The activities in the claim handling process include acknowledging a claim and assigning it to a claim representative, identifying the policy, contacting the insured or the insured's representative, investigating and documenting the claim, determining cause of loss and loss amount, and concluding the claim. A basic understanding of these claim handling activities helps insurance professionals understand how an insurer complies with the contractual promise made in the insurance policy.

A variety of claim personnel collaborate to fulfill the contractual promise that insurers make to their insureds in insurance policies. Claim managers oversee various levels of the claim operation. Claim supervisors support the claim functions of the managers to whom they report. Claim representatives, including telephone claim representatives, field claim representatives, and technical specialists, investigate, evaluate, and settle claims. Customer service representatives perform routine processing and clerical tasks and may handle routine claims. Producers assist their insurance clients by recording claims and sometimes settle small claims.

An insurer's claim results help determine its success. Insurers can evaluate claim results through financial measures and nonfinancial measures. Financial measures include the insurer's loss ratio, expense ratio, and reserving accuracy. These measures reflect how claims are investigated, negotiated, and paid; the expenses of claim handling; and the accuracy of reserves. (Other insurer functions also affect the loss ratio and expense ratio.) Nonfinancial measures help an insurer evaluate both the claim function and the performance of individual claim representatives.

Direct Your Learning

Insurance Coverage

Educational Objectives

After learning the content of this chapter and completing the corresponding course guide assignment, you should be able to:

▸ Explain how insurance policies can be structured.

▸ Identify common insurance policy provisions and the purpose of each.

▸ Explain how to read an insurance policy to determine whether a claim is covered.

Outline

Physical Structure of Insurance Policies

Common Policy Provisions

Policy Analysis

Summary

Insurance Coverage

PHYSICAL STRUCTURE OF INSURANCE POLICIES

An insurance policy is a carefully written contract that describes the agreement between the insured individual or group and the insurer that provides coverage for unforeseen and accidental losses. In addition to describing what it covers, the policy must describe the coverage's limitations, restrictions, and exclusions clearly so that both parties understand their obligations.

When an accident or a loss occurs, the insurer determines whether the policy covers the loss and, if so, the dollar amount the insurer will pay. The insured participates to some extent in determining coverage.

Familiarity with insurance policy structure and content helps insurance professionals analyze a policy's terms. Insurance policy physical structure can vary depending on customer coverage needs. Policies may be on preprinted (standard or nonstandard) forms, or they may be in manuscript form, written for insureds with unique coverage needs.

Some policies address complete coverage needs and are therefore **self-contained policies**; other policies, called **modular policies**, require more than one form or document to address all coverage needs. Documents in modular policies may be attached to the policy or may be incorporated by reference into the policy.

Preprinted and Manuscript Forms

Depending on whether the insurer can use a form already created or must create a new form for a client, the policy can be either a preprinted form or a manuscript form.

Most insurers use standard preprinted policy forms because it is not necessary to negotiate new contractual terms for each policy purchased. Insurance advisory organizations, such as Insurance Services Office (ISO) and American Association of Insurance Services (AAIS), develop industry-wide standardized forms for different types of insurance, and many insurers use these standard forms for insureds who purchase particular coverages. Alternatively, an insurer may develop its own nonstandard, preprinted form.

When using preprinted forms, whether standard or nonstandard, insurers provide insureds with the policies themselves, along with declarations pages indicating the form numbers and edition dates for those policies. For example, a person buying auto insurance may find that three or four smaller insurers all

Self-contained policy
A single document that contains all the agreements between the insured and the insurer and that forms a complete insurance policy.

Modular policy
An insurance policy that consists of several different documents, none of which by itself forms a complete policy.

are using an ISO standard policy form, but that one large insurer is using its own nonstandard policy form for auto coverage.

A **manuscript policy** is a customized contract developed for a specific insured or group of insureds who share unique coverage needs. For example, an insurer might develop a manuscript policy to meet an explosives manufacturer's specific property coverage needs. Because of the limited number of insureds requiring this coverage, insurers typically would not have standard forms available that would cover this exposure.

> **Manuscript policy**
> Nonstandard, custom policies developed for one specific insured or for a small group of insureds, such as a business association, with unique coverage needs.

Self-Contained and Modular Policies

Depending on the type and variety of coverage a customer seeks, a policy can be a single document (self-contained), or it may require a number of documents to include all the agreements between the insured and the insurer (modular).

If the customer seeks coverage that is common to a large number of insureds, the insurer may choose to offer a self-contained policy. A personal auto policy is an example of a self-contained policy. Because most drivers have very similar auto insurance needs, a self-contained policy would serve the needs of most insureds.

Conversely, if the customer seeks a variety of coverages that may not be common to a large number of insureds, the insurer may choose to offer a modular policy to tailor a policy to an insured's specific needs.

A commercial package policy (CPP) is an example of a modular policy because it combines different forms, depending on an insured's needs. Commercial insureds' needs vary, depending on the type of business insured. For example, some businesses may need commercial auto coverage, and others may not.

An insured elects coverages by choosing a limit of liability and premium stated in the declarations and can decline other coverage.

All commercial package policies begin with two components: common policy conditions and common **declarations**. Adding the necessary forms to make up an individual coverage part that meets the insured's specific needs completes the policy. In most cases, a separate declarations page is included for each insurance coverage the CPP provides.

> **Declarations**
> An insurance policy information page or pages providing specific details about the insured and the subject of the insurance.

Related Documents

Several related documents can become part of a policy in two ways: they can be physically attached, or they can be referred to within, or incorporated by reference into, the policy.

Insurance Coverage

Components of the ISO CPP

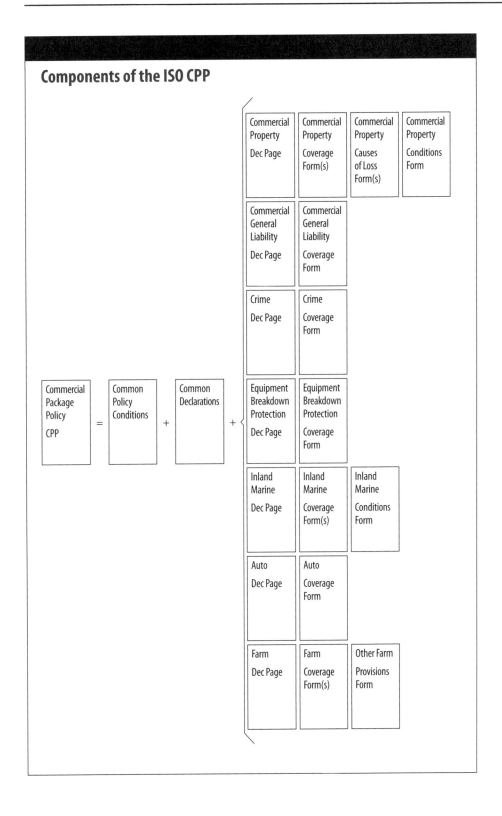

Examples of documents that can become part of a policy are the completed application, endorsements, the insurer's bylaws, relevant statutory terms or provisions, and miscellaneous other documents.

Related Insurance Policy Documents

Related document	Description	Example
Application	Documented request for coverage, containing information about insured and loss exposures	Personal auto policy application containing relevant insured information pertinent to driving and vehicle/s
Endorsements	Documents modifying basic policy form that can differ from basic policy terms	Homeowners policy for home business coverage
Insurer's bylaws	Insurer's corporate bylaws	Mutual policy giving insureds corporate rights
Relevant statutory terms	Incorporation of statute by reference in policy	Workers compensation or no-fault auto insurance statutes
Miscellaneous documents	Documents not included in other categories above	Premium notes, inspection reports, specification sheets, operating manuals

An insurance application, the documented request for coverage, contains information about the insured and the loss exposures presented to the insurer. Underwriters and raters use the application to price the policy.

The insurer usually keeps the completed application in order to preserve the insured's representations. In some cases, misleading or false representations in an application can be grounds for denying a claim. Some state statutes require that any written application become part of the policy for some types of insurance.

Another type of document that can form part of a policy is the endorsements. An **endorsement** adds to, deletes, replaces, or modifies an insurance policy. An endorsement may be a few words handwritten into a policy, or it may be on a separate page—preprinted, computer-printed, typewritten, or handwritten—that is attached to one of the documents forming the policy.

An endorsement's provisions may differ from the provisions of the basic policy to which the endorsement is attached. If the policy and the endorsement contain conflicting terms, the endorsement takes precedence. Agreements

Endorsement
A document that amends an insurance policy.

between an insurer and insured, particularly handwritten alterations, tend to reflect true intent more accurately than do other, preprinted policy terms.

Some insurance contracts incorporate the insurer's bylaws or pertinent statutory provisions. For example, mutual and reciprocal insurance policyholders typically have rights and duties associated with managing the insurer's operations; the policy specifies these rights and duties by incorporating corporate documents.

Policies providing workers compensation insurance or auto no-fault insurance are among those that provide benefits required by state statutes. The insurance policy usually does not contain the relevant statutes but incorporates them by reference. For example, a standard workers compensation policy issued by the National Council on Compensation Insurance (NCCI) notes:

> Workers' compensation law means the workers or workmen's compensation law and occupational disease law of each state or territory named in Item 3.A. of the Information Page. It includes any amendments to that law which are in effect during the policy period.

Some frequently used miscellaneous documents include premium notes (promissory notes accepted by the insurer in lieu of a cash premium payment), inspection reports, and specification sheets or operating manuals relating to safety equipment or procedures. For example, coverage provided by a particular property or liability insurance policy may be conditioned on the use of certain procedures or safety equipment. Operating instructions or a manual of specifications can be incorporated into the policy by reference to precisely define the agreed-upon procedures or equipment.

States often require insurers to provide a "notice to policyholders" informing insureds of significant changes in an insurance policy after the contract has been finalized. In other cases, insurers must furnish policyholders with documents summarizing the coverage options available to insureds. These documents generally do not become part of the policy.

COMMON POLICY PROVISIONS

Policy provisions are insurance policy statements communicating the details of the insurer's and insured's coverage agreements. They describe and clarify the insurance policy's coverage, the types of losses the policy does not cover, and the parties' contractual responsibilities.

Each policy provision typically fits within one of six categories, depending on the provision's purpose. Some policy provisions appear in policy sections matching the provision's category, such as a definition located in the policy's definitions section. Other policy provisions may be interspersed throughout the policy.

Policy provision
Any phrase or clause in an insurance policy that describes the policy's coverages, exclusions, limits, conditions, or other features.

Common policy provisions fall within six categories:

- Declarations
- Definitions
- Insuring agreements
- Conditions
- Exclusions
- Miscellaneous provisions

Categories of Property-Casualty Insurance Policy Conditions

Category	Description	Effect on Coverage
Declarations	Unique information on the insured; list of forms included in policy	Outline who or what is covered, and where and when coverage applies
Definitions	Words with special meanings in policy	May limit or expand coverage based on definitions of terms
Insuring Agreements	Promise to make payment	Outline circumstances under which the insurer agrees to pay
Conditions	Qualifications on promise to make payment	Outline steps insured needs to take to enforce policy
Exclusions	Limitations on promise to make payment	Limit insurer's payments based on excluded persons, places, things, or actions
Miscellaneous Provisions	Wide variety of provisions that may alter policy	Deal with the relationship between the insured and the insurer or establish procedures for implementing the policy

Declarations

An insurance policy first must identify the parties to the contract. Information specific to the policy, such as the insurer's and insured's names and locations and the subject of insurance, usually appear on the policy's first page, usually called the declarations page, or declarations, or dec.

The purpose of the declarations is to personalize a preprinted policy and tailor it to fit a particular policyholder's needs. The declarations contain (declare) information about the insured from the insurance application. They also describe the insurer's statement of the coverage provided under the policy, along with other information unique to the policy.

The declarations page typically contains this information:

- Policy number
- Policy inception and expiration dates
- Insurer's name
- Producer's name
- Named insured (policyholder)
- Named insured's mailing address
- Physical address and description of covered property or operations
- Numbers and edition dates of all attached forms and endorsements
- Dollar amounts of applicable policy limits
- Dollar amounts of applicable deductibles
- Names of persons or organizations whose additional interests the policy covers (such as mortgagees, loss payees, or additional insureds)
- Premium amount
- Any optional coverages the applicant has chosen

Policy forms or endorsements also may contain information that qualifies as declarations, often in the form of **scheduled coverage**. For example, a homeowner might want increased limits of theft coverage for antique silverware stored in the home. A policy endorsement would list the details for such increased limits in a personal property schedule.

Scheduled coverage
Insurance for property specifically listed (scheduled) on a policy, with a limit of liability for each item.

Definitions

Many insurance policies contain a definitions section defining policy terms to help clarify real or perceived ambiguity. This section can appear anywhere in the policy; it is usually near the beginning of personal lines policies, such as homeowners or auto policies, and near the end of commercial lines policies.

A policy's definitions section defines words and expressions having specific meaning within the policy. In some policies, defined words may appear in boldface or within quotation marks every time the policy uses them with the specified meaning.

Homeowners Policy Declarations

Homeowners Policy Declarations

POLICYHOLDER: David M. and Joan G. Smith
(Named Insured) 216 Brookside Drive
Anytown, USA 40000

POLICY NUMBER: 296 H 578661

POLICY PERIOD: **Inception:** March 30, 2008
Expiration: March 30, 2009

Policy period begins 12:01 A.M. standard time at the residence premises.

FIRST MORTGAGEE AND MAILING ADDRESS:

Federal National Mortgage Assn.
C/O Mortgagee, Inc.
P.O. Box 5000
Businesstown, USA 55000

We will provide the insurance described in this policy in return for the premium and compliance with all applicable policy provisions.

SECTION I COVERAGES	LIMIT	
A—Dwelling	$ 120,000	**SECTION I DEDUCTIBLE:** $ 250
B—Other Structures	$ 12,000	(In case of loss under Section I, we cover
C—Personal Property	$ 60,000	only that part of the loss over the
D—Loss of Use	$ 36,000	deductible amount shown above.)

SECTION II COVERAGES	LIMIT	
E—Personal Liability	$ 300,000	Each Occurrence
F—Medical Payments to Others	$ 1,000	Each Person

CONSTRUCTION: Masonry Veneer   **NO. FAMILIES:** One   **TYPE ROOF:** Approved

YEAR BUILT: 1990   **PROTECTION CLASS:** 7   **FIRE DISTRICT:** Cook Township

NOT MORE THAN 1000 FEET FROM HYDRANT

NOT MORE THAN 5 MILES FROM FIRE DEPT.

FORMS AND ENDORSEMENTS IN POLICY: HO 00 03, HO 04 61

POLICY PREMIUM: $ 350.00   **COUNTERSIGNATURE DATE:** March 1, 2008   **AGENT:** A.M. Abel

Insurers and courts interpret undefined policy terms under these contract interpretation rules:

- Commonly used words are given their standard dictionary meanings.
- Technical words are given their technical meanings.
- Words with an established legal meaning are given their legal meanings.
- Words having local, cultural, and trade-usage meanings are considered to have those meanings in a policy.

Insuring Agreements

The purpose of a policy insuring agreement, which often follows the declarations and sometimes follows the definitions section, is to state in broad terms the insurer's promises to the insured. An **insuring agreement** is any policy statement indicating that the insurer will pay for a loss or provide a service under described circumstances. A policy providing more than one coverage can have more than one insuring agreement. For example, the Personal Auto Policy (PAP) typically provides liability, medical payments, uninsured motorists, and physical damage coverages, and each coverage has its own insuring agreement.

An insuring agreement usually introduces a coverage section, but it also can introduce other policy sections, such as coverage extensions, additional coverages, and supplementary payments.

An insuring agreement introducing a coverage section broadly states what the insurer agrees to do under the policy, subject to clarification in other parts of the policy, such as the policy definitions. Insuring agreements usually contain one or more defined terms crucial to understanding the coverage.

Insuring agreement
A statement in an insurance policy that the insurer will, under described circumstances, make a loss payment or provide a service.

Conditions

A policy **condition** is any provision qualifying an insurer's promise or an insured's duty. A policy's conditions section clarifies the insurer's and insured's duties, rights, and options. Some policy conditions are included in a policy's conditions section; others may be found in the forms, endorsements, or other documents that together form the entire insurance policy.

The insured must comply with conditions for a policy to cover a loss. The insurer is obligated only if the insured has fulfilled its contractual duties as specified in the policy conditions.

The insurer's obligations, as stated in the insuring agreement, may include these duties:

- To pay covered losses
- To defend the insured from lawsuits
- To provide other services to the insured

Condition
Any provision in an insurance policy that qualifies an otherwise enforceable promise of the insurer.

These are the insured's obligations, which stem from the policy conditions:

- To pay premiums
- To report losses promptly
- To provide appropriate documentation for losses
- To cooperate with the insurer, as in legal proceedings, for example
- To refrain from jeopardizing an insurer's rights to recover from responsible third parties (subrogate)

If the insured fails to perform these duties, the insurer may be released from its policy obligations.

Exclusions

Exclusions are policy provisions that state what the insurer will not cover. The primary function of exclusions is not only to limit coverage but also to clarify the coverages granted by the insurer.

An exclusion can serve one or more purposes:

- Eliminate coverage for uninsurable loss exposures—Some loss exposures are not generally insurable. Exclusions allow insurers to eliminate coverage for nonaccidental events such as war, earthquake, or flood damage to fixed-location property, and normal wear and tear.
- Assist in managing moral hazards—Exaggerated or intentionally caused losses for the purpose of collecting insurance proceeds may be the result of **moral hazards**. Exclusions help insurers minimize loss exposures that moral hazards affect.
- Assist in managing morale hazards—Losses often arise from carelessness or indifference because an individual is insured, reflecting **morale**, or **attitudinal, hazards**. Exclusions help insurers minimize loss exposures that morale hazards affect.
- Reduce likelihood of coverage duplications—Sometimes two types of insurance policies may cover the same loss. Exclusions ensure that policies work together to provide complementary, but not duplicate, coverages.
- Eliminate coverages that the typical insured does not need—Exclusions can allow insurers to exclude coverage for loss exposures that typical insureds do not face. These exclusions eliminate the possibility that all insureds would have to share the costs of covering substantial loss exposures of relatively few insureds. For example, a policy might exclude coverage for destruction of a motorboat, because many insureds do not own motorboats. Watercraft policies or endorsements can provide coverage for this loss exposure.

Exclusion
A policy provision that eliminates coverage for specified exposures.

Moral hazard
A condition that increases the likelihood that a person will intentionally cause or exaggerate a loss.

Morale, or attitudinal, hazard
A condition of carelessness or indifference that increases the frequency or severity of loss.

- Eliminate coverages requiring special treatment—These coverages might require rating, underwriting, loss control, or other treatment that differs from that normally applied to the policy. An example is workers compensation coverage.
- Assist in keeping premiums reasonable—Exclusions allow insurers to decline loss exposures that would increase overall insurance costs. By excluding such loss exposures, insurers can offer less costly premiums.

Exclusions typically appear in the exclusions section of the policy, but other policy sections, such as insuring agreements, may also refer to them.

Miscellaneous Provisions

Insurance policies often contain miscellaneous provisions that do not qualify strictly as declarations, definitions, insuring agreements, exclusions, or conditions. Miscellaneous provisions may deal with the relationship between the insured and the insurer or help establish procedures for implementing the policy. Miscellaneous provisions may affect coverage but do not have the force of conditions. Consequently, if the insured does not follow procedures specified in miscellaneous provisions, the insurer typically still must fulfill its contractual promises.

An example of a miscellaneous provision is a description of standards the insurer uses when determining the value of a loss, such as basing the value of an auto on the National Automobile Dealers Association (NADA) Blue Book. Miscellaneous provisions also may be unique to a particular type of insurer, such as a mutual insurer, in which policyholders have voting rights. In this case, one miscellaneous provision might describe the policyholders' right to elect the board of directors.

POLICY ANALYSIS

A common goal in analyzing an insurance policy is determining the answers to these two questions:

- Does the policy cover the loss?
- What dollar amount will the insurer pay?

Policy analysis is most efficient when the questions are considered sequentially.

Does the Policy Cover the Loss?

Verifying policy coverage can take place either before a loss (pre-loss) or after a loss (post-loss). Pre-loss determinations, which can be difficult, usually arise in response to "what-if" questions from an applicant for insurance or an insured. Two methods used for post-loss policy analysis are the question-and-answer method and the "DICE" method.

Insurable interest
An interest in the subject of an insurance policy that is not unduly remote and that would cause the interested party to suffer financial loss if an insured event occurred.

Question-and-Answer Method

Using the question-and-answer method of analysis can help determine whether a policy covers a loss. Those analyzing the policy should answer these questions:

- Does an enforceable insurance policy exist?
- Did an insured party who has an **insurable interest** incur the loss?
- Has the insured met all of the policy conditions?
- Has an insured event occurred?

If the answer to each of these questions is yes, the loss is covered, and analysis continues to determine how much is payable under the policy. If the answer to any of the questions is no, the loss is not covered, and policy analysis is complete.

DICE Method

The DICE method of policy analysis to determine coverage creates a decision tree to review of categories of policy provisions.

The DICE acronym represents four of the six sections of a property-casualty insurance policy: declarations, insuring agreement, conditions, and exclusions. The other two sections of a policy are definitions and miscellaneous provisions. While the DICE acronym represents only four of the six categories of policy provisions, all six categories are analyzed in this method, including the definitions and miscellaneous provisions categories.

Declarations—Review of the declarations page can verify whether any information, such as policy inception and expiration dates, precludes coverage. If not, the analysis moves on to the insuring agreement.

Insuring agreement—The insuring agreement often contains provisions regarding covered property or events, covered causes of loss, and coverage territories. Analyzing definitions is also part of this step. If nothing in the insuring agreement or definitions precludes coverage, the analysis proceeds to the policy conditions.

Conditions—Policy conditions specify the insurer's and the insured's duties. Failure to fulfill a condition can preclude coverage of an otherwise-covered claim. For example, a common condition requires the insured to provide timely notice of a loss to the insurer. Another common condition requires the insured to pay a premium before the policy becomes enforceable. If a loss occurs before the insured has paid the premium, the insurer has no obligation to pay the claim. If all conditions have been fulfilled, the analysis continues to the policy's exclusions.

Exclusions—Exclusions can appear anywhere in the policy, as well as in the policy's exclusions section; therefore, analysis of exclusions must include any categories of policy provisions that were not previously evaluated. These can include exclusions, endorsements, miscellaneous provisions, and other related documents that are part of the policy.

Although the DICE acronym represents only four of the six categories of policy provisions, the entire policy must be examined for provisions that might affect coverage.

What Dollar Amount Will the Insurer Pay?

Once it has been determined that the loss is covered, the next task is to determine how much the insurer should pay. Many insurance provisions, including policy limits, deductibles, and self-insured retentions, can affect the amount payable under a policy, and those provisions vary with the type of policy.

For property insurance, the amount payable is influenced by a policy's valuation provision, which designates whether covered property will be valued on the basis of its replacement cost, its depreciated actual cash value, or some other basis. Additionally, a deductible might apply to the amount payable. For liability insurance, the courts, or more commonly, a negotiated settlement, can determine the amount payable.

Other insurance or noninsurance recovery sources can also affect the amounts payable for both property and liability insurance losses. For example, a policyholder might recover part or all of a loss by suing another party.

SUMMARY

An insurance policy's physical structure depends on the coverage or customer. Insurers use standard or manuscript forms, and polices may be either self-contained or modular. Modular polices contain multiple documents, which may either be attached to the policy or incorporated by reference.

Common policy provisions communicate the details of an insurer's and an insured's agreements as to coverage. They fall within six categories: declarations, definitions, insuring agreements, conditions, exclusions, and miscellaneous provisions.

Declarations personalize a printed policy, tailoring it to fit a policyholder's needs. A definitions section defines words and expressions having specific meaning within the policy. An insuring agreement states an insurer's promises broadly. A condition is any provision qualifying an otherwise enforceable insurer's promise or insured's duty. The exclusions state what the insurer does not intend to cover. Miscellaneous provisions, which do not qualify as declarations, definitions, insuring agreements, exclusions, or conditions, may affect coverage but do not have the force of conditions.

Analyzing an insurance policy involves determining whether the policy covers a loss and, if so, what dollar amount the insurer will pay.

To determine whether the policy covers the loss, those analyzing the policy can use either the question-and-answer method or the DICE method of policy analysis. Determining what dollar amount the insurer will pay requires analysis of policy provisions such as policy limits, deductibles, and self-insured retentions.

For property insurance, the valuation provision in a policy is important for determining the amount payable. For liability insurance, courts or negotiated settlements can determine the amount payable. Other insurance or noninsurance recovery sources also can affect amounts payable for either property or liability losses.

Direct Your Learning

Personal Insurance

Educational Objectives

After learning the content of this chapter and completing the corresponding course guide assignment, you should be able to:

▸ Identify the common property and liability loss exposures of individuals and families.

▸ Identify the coverage provided by a homeowners insurance policy and the loss exposures this policy protects against.

▸ Identify the coverage provided by a personal auto insurance policy and the loss exposures the policy protects against.

▸ Identify the coverage provided by the following personal insurance policies and the loss exposures each protects against:

- Dwelling insurance
- Personal umbrella insurance
- Personal inland marine insurance
- Flood insurance

Outline

Personal Property and Liability Loss Exposures

Homeowners Insurance Policy

Personal Auto Insurance Policy

Other Personal Insurance Policies

Summary

Personal Insurance

PERSONAL PROPERTY AND LIABILITY LOSS EXPOSURES

All individuals and families face loss exposures. Personal loss exposures, which include property and liability loss exposures, typically arise from the property that individuals and families own, such as homes, contents of homes, and the ownership and operation of automobiles.

A **property loss exposure** exists when property can be destroyed, damaged, stolen, lost, or otherwise suffer a decrease in value because of a particular **cause of loss** (or peril). Fire is one example of a peril; theft and burglary are others.

Two types of property that are exposed to loss are **real property** and **personal property**. Real property includes land, buildings on the land, and anything growing on the land, such as crops. Personal property includes the contents of a dwelling (for example, furniture, appliances, and clothing), highly valued property (for example, jewelry, silverware, firearms, and artwork), and even property such as autos, trailers, and watercraft.

Examples of common property loss exposures include these:

- Fire damage to a house caused by excess growth of nearby shrubbery that alights during wildfire season
- Snow and ice damage requiring a home's roof shingles to be replaced
- Fire damage to a field of winter wheat that is struck by lightning
- Wind damage to a fence surrounding a built-in swimming pool
- Water damage to the contents of a home caused by a burst pipe
- Theft of property, including jewelry or silverware, belonging to an individual or a family
- Collision damage to an automobile caused by an auto accident
- Total loss of a sailboat that breaks loose from its moorings during a storm and sinks

Property loss exposure
A condition that presents the possibility that a person or an organization will sustain a loss resulting from damage (including destruction, taking, or loss of use) to property in which that person or organization has a financial interest.

Cause of loss
The actual means by which property is damaged or destroyed.

Real property
Tangible property consisting of land, all structures permanently attached to the land, and whatever is growing on the land.

Personal property
All tangible or intangible property that is not real property.

> **Personal Loss Exposures—An Example**
>
> How individuals and families treat personal insurance loss exposures varies widely. First, there must be an awareness of the loss exposure. For example, consider Julio, who has lived in his current home for approximately ten years. He may not realize that a severe summer storm has removed shingles from his roof, presenting a loss exposure that will only worsen until the damage is discovered (perhaps when another severe storm occurs). Only then may Julio address the loss exposure, the damaged shingles. Second, once there is an awareness of a loss exposure, it can be treated it in a variety of ways.

Liability Loss Exposures

Liability loss exposure
Any condition or situation that presents the possibility of a claim alleging legal responsibility of a person or business for injury or damage suffered by another party.

Personal **liability loss exposures** typically arise from an individual or a family's ownership of property or from their actions. For example, anything on an individual's property that presents the possibility of someone tripping and falling, such as uneven pavement or an exposed tree stump, is a liability loss exposure. Other common liability loss exposures associated with real property include an improperly fenced swimming pool or a secondary home occupied by tenants.

An example of a common liability loss exposure arising from personal property ownership is possession of a dog known to bite. Additionally, an individual can be sued if found to be liable for property damage or bodily injury caused by an automobile collision. Also, liability loss exposures can arise from the operation of a boat and can include such incidents as collision with other watercraft or bodily injury to another boater.

Personal liability loss exposures also can arise from an individual or a family's actions. Any individual's or family member's actions that cause bodily injury to another party or damage to someone else's property can constitute a liability loss exposure. For example, a child could throw a rock through a neighbor's window or break a car window while playing baseball in the street.

The primary manner in which property owners treat loss exposures is by purchasing insurance. Insurance addresses most of the property and liability loss exposures that can arise as a consequence of home ownership or ownership of personal property.

HOMEOWNERS INSURANCE POLICY

Homeowners insurance policies provide property and liability coverage for many personal loss exposures.

Package policy
Policy that covers two or more lines of business.

Homeowners insurance policies are **package policies** that combine property insurance and liability insurance coverage in a single policy designed to meet the various insurance needs of individuals and families. These package policies are the primary way in which individuals and families who own property address their various loss exposures.

A homeowners policy offers individuals and families these primary features:

- Coverage for property and liability loss exposures
- Choice of policy forms and covered perils

Applicants can select, from among the various homeowners insurance policy forms, the ones that provide them with the coverages and covered perils that best suit them.

Homeowners coverage includes insurance for the real property, personal property, and personal liability loss exposures that arise as a consequence of home ownership. Real property loss exposures covered include a dwelling and anything growing on land. Personal property loss exposures covered can include the contents of a dwelling (such as furniture, appliances, and clothing), highly valued property (such as jewelry, silverware, firearms, and artwork), and such property as trailers and watercraft. Personal liability loss exposures that individuals and families typically face include those related to an insured's ownership of property and to the insured's personal activities.

Coverage for Property and Liability Loss Exposures

A homeowners policy contains coverage for certain property and liability loss exposures. Under a typical policy offered by **Insurance Services Office (ISO)**, whose policy forms serve as the basis of this discussion (additional organizations also supply policy forms for insurer use), property coverages are found under the portion of the policy called Section I coverages, and liability coverages are found under the portion of the policy called Section II coverages. Each section contains insuring agreements describing specific coverages, as well as related policy conditions and exclusions. Homeowners policies also have a declarations page providing details about the policy coverage.

Insurance Services Office (ISO)
An advisory organization that provides analytical and decision-support products and services to the property-liability insurance industry.

Section I – Property Coverages

Section I of a homeowners policy provides these primary property coverages:

- Dwelling
- Other Structures
- Personal Property
- Loss of Use

Dwelling coverage insures an insured's dwelling (the house itself). Coverage also extends to any structures attached to the house, such as an attached garage or carport. A homeowners insurance policy can protect against loss exposures such as fire damage to the dwelling, wind damage to the dwelling's roof, or smoke damage to the dwelling's interior kitchen walls.

Other Structures coverage provides coverage on an insured's other structures located on the residence premises. Structures that are not attached to the house are also covered by a homeowners policy. To be eligible for coverage, other structures must be separated from the house by a clear space or fence. Examples of other structures include a detached garage, swimming pool, fence, or utility shed. A homeowners insurance policy can protect against loss exposures such as fire damage to a detached garage, lightning damage to a swimming pool, or fire damage to a fence.

Personal Property coverage insures all of an insured's property other than real estate (the house) and typically includes the contents of the residence, such as clothing, furniture, and appliances. If the property is not permanently installed in the dwelling's foundation or in the home itself, it is usually considered personal property. A homeowners policy can protect against loss exposures such as water damage to rugs if a pipe bursts, damage to furniture after a fire, or theft of jewelry.

Loss of Use coverage provides coverage to an insured for periods during which the insured residence is rendered uninhabitable by a covered loss. For example, a home that has sustained major fire damage usually is not suitable for residency while it is being repaired. One benefit of Loss of Use coverage is that the insurer covers the loss exposure of any increase in living expenses the insured incurs as a consequence of a loss, such as hotel expenses. Another benefit of Loss of Use coverage is that the insurer covers the **fair rental value** of the loss if the portion of the home that was damaged (eligible under a homeowners form) was rented to a tenant.

Fair rental value
Under Coverage D - Loss of Use of a homeowners policy, the amount of rent (less any discontinued expenses) that the insured would have received for the residence or any part of the residence rented to another individual for residential purposes, if the residence had not been damaged.

Section II – Liability Coverages

Section II of a homeowners policy provides these liability coverages:

- Personal Liability
- Medical Payments to Others

Personal Liability coverage provides coverage for claims for bodily injury or property damage for which the insured is legally liable. Personal Liability coverage is usually purchased with a limit of liability of $300,000 or more. The limit applies to each claim (occurrence), and the insurer has an obligation to defend the insured against claims and the right to conduct a legal defense on the insured's behalf. For example, the Personal Liability section of a homeowners policy covers an insured who is sued as a consequence of a delivery person tripping and falling on the insured's sidewalk, and it would also cover the damages resulting from an insured's young child hitting a baseball through a neighbor's living room window.

Medical Payments to Others coverage provides coverage for any necessary medical payments incurred by others (not insureds) within three years of the loss date. This coverage often is considered accident or goodwill coverage because it does not require that the insured be legally liable for the bodily injury requiring the medical payments. Because of the nature of the coverage, limits commonly are selected that are lower than personal liability limits (limits of $1,000 or $2,000 are typical). For example, if a guest helping an insured hostess put away dishes after a diner cuts his finger on a knife and requires stitches, medical payments coverage would cover the cost of the stitches, up to the policy limit.

Choice of Policy Forms and Covered Perils

ISO offers individuals and families a choice of policy forms to meet their loss exposure needs. The differences between the forms lie in which perils are covered under Section I. While there is one particular array of potential loss exposures for which a customer may need the insurance, the customer can vary the perils or causes of loss (based on form selected) used to address them.

Homeowners policy forms all follow a similar general pattern of construction (for example, Section I, Section II) but may vary in terms of coverage specifics. For example, a broad form homeowners policy covers a number of perils under Section I. A special form homeowners policy covers personal property for the same perils as the broad form homeowners policy. However, instead of covering the dwelling and other structures on a named perils basis, the policy covers them on an open perils or risk of direct loss basis, in which any peril that is not specifically excluded is covered. The other homeowners forms also vary in terms of covered perils provided or in their Section I variations.

PERSONAL AUTO INSURANCE POLICY

A personal auto insurance policy is a package policy designed to meet the various automobile insurance needs of individuals and families.

An individual or a family can use a personal auto policy (PAP) to insure an auto against the consequences of losses such as an auto being struck by an at-fault driver (as a collision, or property loss), or that of an insured auto striking and damaging another vehicle (as a liability loss).

Under a typical PAP, insureds can select from a number of coverage options to address the various property and liability loss exposures that may arise from their ownership or operation of an auto.

A PAP offers individuals and families these primary coverages:

- Liability coverage
- Medical payments coverage
- Uninsured motorists coverage
- Physical damage coverage

Homeowners Policy Forms and Covered Perils

Policy Form	Coverage Provided	Covered Perils
HO-2 Broad Form	This form provides coverage for owner-occupants of dwellings. It insures Section I coverages on a named perils basis and provides Section II coverage.	Fire or lightning; windstorm or hail; explosion; riot or civil commotion; aircraft; vehicles; smoke; vandalism or malicious mischief; theft; volcanic eruption
HO-3 Special Form	This form provides coverage for owner-occupants of dwellings. It insures the dwelling and other structures on an open perils basis and personal property on a named perils basis. Section II coverage is also provided.	Broad Form covered perils, plus: falling objects; weight of ice; snow or sleet, accidental discharge or overflow of water or steam; sudden and accidental tearing apart; cracking, burning, or bulging; freezing; sudden and accidental damage from artificially generated electrical current
HO-4 Contents Broad Form	This form is designed for tenants and other occupants of dwellings or apartments. It insures a tenant's personal property on a named perils basis (no dwelling coverage is included). Section II coverage is also provided.	Broad Form covered perils
HO-5 Comprehensive Form	This form is designed for owner-occupants of dwellings. It provides the broadest coverage of all the homeowners forms. It insures the dwelling, other structures, and personal property on an open perils basis. Loss of use and Section II coverages are also provided.	Open perils on dwelling, other structures, and personal property (loss of use coverage based on loss sustained under Coverages A, B, and C)
HO-6 Unit-Owners Form	This form is designed for the owners of condominiums. It insures personal property on a named perils basis, with limited dwelling coverage (unit improvements and betterments). Loss of Use and Section II coverages are also provided.	Broad Form covered perils
HO-8 Modified Coverage Form	This form is a more limited form of coverage for owner-occupants of dwellings. A valuation clause in the form insures the dwelling, other structures, and personal property, on a limited, named perils basis.	Fire or lightning, windstorm or hail, explosion, riot or civil commotion, aircraft, vehicles, smoke, vandalism or malicious mischief, theft, volcanic eruption

Auto policies also have a declarations page that contains details about the policy coverage. Additionally, PAP coverages are specified in attached insuring agreements. Coverage is further influenced by related policy conditions and exclusions.

Liability Coverage

Liability coverage protects an insured against a claim or lawsuit for bodily injury to pedestrians, occupants of the insured's car, and occupants of other autos, and for property damage to others caused by an insured as a consequence of an auto accident. In order for the liability portion of the policy to pay, the insured must be found legally responsible for the accident. Examples of liability loss exposures include an insured who, while driving, strikes and injures a pedestrian who was legally crossing the street. The pedestrian's injuries would be covered under the bodily injury portion of the insured's PAP liability coverage. Additionally, consider an insured who strikes another vehicle at a traffic light, damaging the other vehicle. The other vehicle's damages would be covered under the property damage portion of the insured's PAP liability coverage, as would any other financial consequences not covered under the other driver's auto policy.

Liability coverage typically is available on either a **single limit basis** or a **split limits basis**. A split limits basis is one in which the amounts of insurance apply separately to bodily injury and property damage. Liability coverage applies to vehicles shown in the declarations and also applies to insureds while they are driving a neighbor's auto or if they rent a car while on vacation. A PAP is intended to cover only occasional use of a nonowned auto. It does not cover insureds while they are driving other cars that are furnished to them or available to them for their regular use. For example, consider the loss exposure of an insured whose employer furnishes a pickup truck to him for his personal use. A PAP would not cover liability for the furnished vehicle.

A PAP also provides coverage to other people who occasionally drive one of the insured's cars. For example, if an insured's neighbor borrowed his or her car, coverage is provided for the loss exposure. Should an accident occur that is the neighbor's fault, the liability portion of the insured's policy would respond.

Medical Payments Coverage

Medical payments coverage pays for the reasonable and necessary medical expenses an insured incurs because of bodily injury caused by an auto accident. Coverage is provided for bodily injury to occupants of the insured's auto if they sustain injuries as the result of an auto accident or while they are entering or exiting the insured's auto. The possibility of individuals being injured while they are occupants of an insured's car or while they are entering or exiting the insured's car are examples of medical payments loss exposures. Coverage also applies to an insured if, as a pedestrian, the insured is struck by another vehicle.

Medical payments coverage is paid without regard to fault. For example, an insured may be driving an auto that is struck by another vehicle whose driver has ignored a traffic signal. Although the other driver is at fault, the insured can be compensated for any injuries sustained as a consequence of the accident under the insured's PAP medical payments coverage.

Coverage is paid on a per-limit, per-person, per-claim basis, regardless of the number of persons involved in the claim. Once the named insured and resident family members exhaust the per-person medical payments limit, they

Single limit basis
One coverage limit that applies to all damages arising from bodily injury or property damage or both, resulting from a single accident.

Split limits basis
Separate coverage limits that allow one limit for bodily injury to each person; a second usually higher limit for bodily injury to all persons in each accident; and a third limit for all property damage in each accident.

typically have no other coverage recourse under a PAP's medical payments coverage or liability coverage. However, if non-family members or family members who are not residents of the insured's household sustain injuries in the insured's vehicle that exceed the medical payments limit, they are allowed to sue or file a liability claim to receive payment for their injuries.

In addition to or as part of the medical payments coverage available with the PAP, many states have enacted laws that allow individuals injured in accidents to collect payments for damages from their own insurers regardless of who is at fault. These laws are known as no-fault laws. There are a number of specific variations in those states that have no-fault laws. True no-fault laws restrict a victim's right to sue a negligent driver. For example, if claims are below a certain monetary threshold, then the accident victims collect only from their own insurers. If claims exceed the monetary threshold amount, then the accident victims can seek payment for damages from negligent drivers and can sue for damages resulting from the accident.

Uninsured Motorists Coverage

Uninsured motorists coverage (UM) pays if an insured incurs bodily injury caused by an uninsured motorist, a hit-and-run driver, or a driver whose insurer is insolvent. The loss exposure is any type of bodily injury sustained by the insured for the uninsured damages.

Consider a case in which the insured driver is struck by a hit-and-run driver. Further assume that the insured's car is deemed a total loss and that the insured sustains injuries of more than $50,000, far in excess of the policy's medical payments limit. If the driver were known, the insured would normally attempt to obtain recovery from the at-fault driver's PAP liability coverage. When an insured has a legal right to recover damages and a source of recovery is not available because of the consequences of the previously described loss exposures, the insured can turn to the PAP uninsured motorist coverage for compensation.

Underinsured motorists coverage (UIM) is an endorsement available under the PAP. It is included automatically with the PAP in some states because it operates closely with uninsured motorists coverage. Underinsured motorists coverage pays if an insured incurs bodily injury caused by an underinsured motorist who is found liable in an accident involving the insured. The loss exposure is any type of bodily injury sustained by the insured for the underinsured damages. The coverage pays the difference between the underinsured motorists coverage limit on the insured's vehicle and the liability limits on the at-fault vehicle (up to the maximum underinsured motorists limit). For example, assume the insured was involved in an accident with another (at-fault) driver who collided with the insured's car. Further assume that the insured sues the at-fault driver for $100,000 of compensation for injuries suffered during the accident. What would the insured's PAP and the at-fault driver's PAP pay for the insured's injuries if the following PAP coverages applied?

These are the available PAP Coverages in this example:

- Insured's liability limit—$300,000 single limit
- Insured's uninsured motorists limit—$100,000 single limit
- Insured's underinsured motorists limit—$100,000 single limit
- At-fault driver's liability limit—$50,000 single limit
- Judgment obtained by insured against at-fault driver—$100,000

The at-fault driver's PAP insurer pays the insured its liability policy limit of $50,000. The at-fault driver does not qualify as an uninsured motorist, so the insured's UM coverage pays nothing. However, the insured's UIM coverage would pay the remaining $50,000 of the damages because the at-fault driver's liability limit was less than the insured's uninsured motorists coverage limit and is within the insured's available UIM limit.

Physical Damage Coverage

Physical damage coverage is property insurance that covers disappearance of, damage to, or destruction of the auto itself. Coverage can apply to an insured's covered auto as well as to certain non-owned autos, less any applicable policy deductible. Loss exposures covered include damage (or the possibility of damage) to the insured's auto and other certain non-owned autos. Non-owned autos can include vehicles borrowed by the insured that are not available for the insured's regular use, or any auto or trailer not owned by the insured that is being used as a temporary substitute for the insured's auto because of issues such as breakdown, servicing, or destruction. For non-owned autos, coverage is excess over other collectible insurance, which means that the PAP physical damage coverage for non-owned autos only begins paying after all other collectible insurance coverages have been exhausted. The auto policy contains two sets of physical damage coverage: other than collision coverage and collision coverage.

Other Than Collision Coverage

Other than collision coverage applies to losses that do not fall within the policy's definition of collision. Auto policies typically do not define what constitutes an other than collision loss. If a loss is not considered collision, then it usually is considered other than collision. Because the coverage is so broad, many insurance practitioners refer to the coverage as comprehensive coverage. A PAP provides examples of causes of loss that illustrate what the policy considers other than collision. These causes of loss include fire, theft, animal contact, flood, and glass breakage. Other than collision loss exposures can consequently include auto theft, water damage due to flood, contact with an animal such as a bird or deer, or fire damage.

Collision Coverage

Collision coverage applies to losses relating to the insured's covered auto striking another auto or an object, or the upset of an insured's covered autos. Collision coverage is an optional coverage under the PAP, and is typically available only when other than collision coverage also is purchased. Collision loss exposures can include vehicle upset as a consequence of operation, collision with another auto, or collision with another object such as a guardrail or building.

> **Other Than Collision Coverage Example**
>
> Linda has just purchased a new sedan. On her way home from the new car dealer, she inadvertently strikes a deer on a rural road, causing $4,500 of damage to the car. When Linda purchased the car, she requested a PAP with a $500 other than collision deductible and a $1,000 collision deductible from her insurance agent. The deer strike is covered under the PAP and is considered an other than collision loss, so Linda will receive a $4,000 payment from her insurer.
>
> ($4,500 - $500 deductible = $4,000 payment.)

OTHER PERSONAL INSURANCE POLICIES

Personal auto policies and homeowners policies adequately address many loss exposures that affect individuals and families. Some loss exposures, however, require additional types of insurance.

Other personal insurance policies are available to meet a variety of personal insurance needs and protect insureds against certain loss exposures arising from property ownership and individual actions. In addition to a basic homeowners and personal auto policy, these policies address personal insurance needs:

- Dwelling insurance
- Personal umbrella insurance
- Personal inland marine insurance
- Flood insurance

Each of these policies typically contains its own declarations page that provides details about the policy coverage. Additionally, the coverages supplied are specified in attached insuring agreements, and coverage is further influenced by related policy conditions and exclusions.

Dwelling Insurance

Some dwellings do not qualify for coverage under homeowners policies. For example, a homeowners policy may not cover a two-family rental dwelling owned by an insured who lives elsewhere in a primary home. Alternatively, a dwelling whose value is below the limit required for a homeowners policy may require other coverage (for example, if an insurer requires a minimum dwelling limit of $50,000 for a new homeowners policy, a building valued at only $40,000 would not qualify). A dwelling also may not be suited to a homeowners policy if the homeowners insurance program places stricter requirements on the number of additional families per unit than does the dwelling program.

Dwelling policies principally insure one- to four-family dwellings, whether they are owner or tenant occupied. Coverage is provided on one of three forms: a limited coverage form (the **Basic Form**, or DP 1), a form providing broader coverage (the **Broad Form**, or DP 2), and a special or "all-risks" coverage form (the **Special Form**, or DP 3). Dwelling policy coverage is more limited and narrower in scope than that provided by homeowners policies. Therefore, premiums for it often are comparatively less costly.

Dwelling insurance provides coverage for the dwelling, other structures, and personal property. It also provides fair rental value coverage. Coverage for limited theft and personal liability is available by endorsement.

An eligible individual or family can obtain coverage for a property by obtaining a dwelling policy for the building's full amount. Additionally, an insured can obtain personal liability coverage via an endorsement to the dwelling insurance policy. An insured who lives elsewhere in a primary home and rents out the dwelling can extend personal liability coverage to the rental property from his or her primary homeowners policy.

Dwelling insurance provides property and liability coverage (based on the form and options selected) for the loss exposures that arise as a consequence of dwelling ownership. Loss exposures covered under a dwelling policy include the consequences of fire damage to an insured's dwelling, wind damage to an insured's roof, or a physical injury incurred by a tenant on the insured's rental property (if personal liability coverage were added to the dwelling policy).

Basic Form
An ISO homeowners form covering a limited number of causes of loss.

Broad Form
An ISO homeowners form covering the same causes of loss as the basic form, plus six additional causes of loss.

Special Form
A policy that provides coverage for any direct loss to property unless the loss is caused by a peril specifically excluded.

Personal Umbrella Insurance

Personal umbrella insurance, or an **umbrella policy**, is a generic term for a broad liability policy intended to provide high liability limits in excess of basic liability policy coverage. Umbrella policies usually have a liability limit of $1 million or more, which is added to the liability limits of an insured's other policies, such as a personal auto policy, a homeowners policy, or a watercraft policy.

If, for example, a catastrophic auto accident occurs whose damages exceed an insured's auto liability limit, the insured's umbrella policy would pay the excess of the loss up to its limit of liability. As another example, assume an individual who trips and falls on an insured's sidewalk subsequently sues the insured and that the judgment is for $500,000 against the insured. The insured's homeowners policy would provide coverage up to its limit (or

Umbrella policy
A policy that provides coverage above underlying policies and may also offer coverage not available in the underlying policies, subject to a self-insured retention.

Personal Umbrella Policy

Personal Liability	$300,000 limit
Personal Auto Liability	$300,000
Watercraft Liability	$500,000
Self-Insured Retention	$250

Personal Umbrella Coverage extends above the underlying limits up to $1,300,000 (for Personal Liability and Personal Auto Liability layers) and up to $1,030,000 above the Watercraft Liability, with Uninsured Exposure above $1,500,000 (and above $1,030,000 for the watercraft column).

"underlying" limit) of liability, and the umbrella policy would pay the excess, equaling the $500,000 judgment total.

Another example of a covered loss exposure applies in a watercraft loss scenario. If an insured boater strikes another boat, causing extensive bodily injury and property damage to the other boater, and the insured is found liable for

$600,000 of damages, the insured's personal watercraft policy would provide coverage up to its limit (or underlying limit) of liability, and the umbrella policy would pay the excess until the $600,000 liability claim was satisfied.

Umbrella policies have broad insuring agreements and relatively few exclusions. Consequently, they cover some types of claims that are excluded or not addressed by a typical basic insurance program. In such cases, a relatively small deductible, called a **self-insured retention** (SIR), applies.

Personal Inland Marine Insurance

An individual or a family may wish to consider purchasing personal **inland marine insurance** for valuable items such as jewelry, silverware, or cameras because of some of these considerations:

- An insurer can tailor coverage to specific types of property (such as jewelry, silverware, or cameras).
- The insured can select appropriate policy limits for items insured, whereas a homeowners policy, for example, sets maximum limits on certain items for theft losses.
- Personal inland marine coverage usually is written on a very broad basis or an "**all-risks**" (risk of direct loss) basis.
- Most personal inland marine policies provide coverage anywhere in the world.
- Insurers usually write personal inland marine insurance without a deductible.

Personal inland marine insurance provides property coverage (based on the form and coverage selected) for any claim for losses that arise as a consequence of ownership of certain types of property.

Loss exposures covered under personal inland marine insurance include the consequences of theft of an insured's jewelry, theft of an insured's coin collection, loss of several pieces of an insured's silverware, or breakage (in a fall) of an insured's camera while on vacation.

Self-insured retention
An amount that is deducted from claims that are payable under an umbrella liability policy and that are not covered at all by any primary policy.

Inland marine insurance
Insurance that covers many different classes of property that typically involve an element of transportation.

"All-risks" policy
An insurance policy that covers any risk of physical loss unless the policy specifically excludes it.

> ### Personal Inland Marine Insurance Overview
> Inland marine insurance developed out of the marine insurance industry of the 1920s. Traditionally, marine insurers wrote coverage for the majority of loss exposures associated with transportation because shippers transported most cargo by sea. As rail and trucking industries developed, marine insurers broadened their coverage to include land loss exposures; hence the term "inland marine." Today, personal inland marine insurance covers property that has a special value or that is frequently moved from one location to another, such as jewelry, furs, cameras, musical instruments, silverware, golf equipment, fine arts, and stamp and coin collections. Coverage is typically sold as an endorsement to a homeowners policy or as an individual policy.

Flood Insurance

A flood is a rising or an overflowing of water onto what is normally dry land. Coverage for the peril of flood is excluded by homeowners policies, dwelling policies, and most other insurance policies that cover property at a fixed location. Flood damage is, however, covered under most auto policies that include physical damage and under most personal inland marine policies.

Some floods cause widespread, catastrophic damage that would create unmanageably large losses for a private insurer that had issued many property policies in the flood area. Therefore, the federal government provides flood insurance through two mechanisms. Insurance can be obtained directly through the National Flood Insurance Program, or a producer may place the business with an insurer that participates in the Federal Insurance Administration's "Write Your Own" program. Eligibility requirements apply to flood insurance's individual building and contents coverage. Communities also must meet eligibility requirements to qualify for the "regular" flood program, which offers better rates and higher building and contents limits than those available in the "emergency" program.

Flood insurance provides property coverage (building and contents) for certain loss exposures that arise as a consequence of property ownership in flood hazard areas. Loss exposures covered under a flood policy include the consequence of flood damage to an insured's building after a river overflows its banks, or destruction of a building's contents if a flood from the same overflowing river sweeps the building and its contents away. An eligible applicant for a single-family dwelling in a community eligible for the "regular" flood program may be able to obtain the flood program maximum limits of $250,000 building coverage and $100,000 maximum contents coverage for the dwelling.

SUMMARY

All individuals and families face personal loss exposures. A personal loss exposure, which can be a property or a liability loss exposure, is any condition that presents the possibility of loss, whether or not a loss occurs. The primary manner in which individuals and families treat the majority of property and liability loss exposures that arise as a consequence of owning property is by purchasing insurance.

Homeowners insurance includes coverage for both property coverages (Section I), including dwelling, other structures, personal property, and loss of use, and liability coverages (Section II), including personal liability and medical payments to others. Homeowners insurance offers individuals and families a choice of policy forms and covered perils designed to treat a variety of loss exposures and meet customer needs.

A personal auto insurance policy combines property insurance and liability insurance coverage in a single policy. Personal auto insurance loss exposures, which include property and liability loss exposures, are any condition that presents the possibility of loss, whether or not an actual loss occurs. A typical personal auto policy (PAP) allows insureds to select from among various coverages, including liability, medical payments, uninsured/underinsured motorists, and physical damage, to address their various property and liability loss exposures.

Many individuals and families require additional types of insurance coverage besides basic homeowners and auto policies to address their various loss exposures. These personal insurance policies include dwelling insurance, personal umbrella insurance, personal inland marine insurance, and flood insurance.

Direct Your Learning

Chapter 8

Commercial Property Insurance

Educational Objectives

After learning the content of this chapter and completing the corresponding course guide assignment, you should be able to:

▶ Identify the common property loss exposures of commercial insureds in terms of the following:

- Types of property
- Causes of loss
- Financial consequences

▶ Identify the coverage provided by the following types of commercial property insurance and the loss exposures each protects against:

- Property insurance on buildings
- Property insurance on personal property
- Inland marine insurance
- Business income insurance

Outline

Commercial Property Loss Exposures

Commercial Property Insurance Coverage

Summary

Commercial Property Insurance

COMMERCIAL PROPERTY LOSS EXPOSURES

Commercial property loss exposures can be identified in terms of types of property, causes of loss, and financial consequences.

For example, if a neighborhood retail store sustains major damage in a fire, the consequences of the loss extend beyond the building itself. In addition to incurring the costs of rebuilding the damaged structure, the store's owners may incur expenses related to the loss of the building's contents, cleanup costs, fire department charges, and income they lost while the store was closed. They also may incur extra expenses to reestablish the business.

All of these considerations relate to components of a property loss exposure. Three important aspects of property loss exposures are:

- The types of property that might be exposed to loss, damage, or destruction
- The causes of loss that might result in property being lost, damaged, or destroyed
- The financial consequences of a property loss

Insurance professionals often identify property loss exposures in terms of these three elements. For example, an insurance professional might speak of a building exposure (type of property), a windstorm exposure (cause of loss), or a loss of business income exposure (financial consequence). Similarly, a property loss exposure could be identified more specifically in terms of two or even all three of these elements, such as a building fire exposure or loss of business income resulting from breakdown of a production machine.

Types of Property

Property is any item with value. Individuals, families, and organizations own and use property, depend on it as a source of income or services, and rely on its value. Property can decline in value—or even become worthless—if it is lost, damaged, or destroyed.

Any item of property can be classified as either real property or personal property. It is important for a businessowner to consider all property loss exposures that could affect the business, even if some of them (such as land) typically are uninsurable.

Real Property

Examples of real property, in addition to land, are buildings, driveways, sidewalks, underground piping, and radio transmission towers. A building consists of more than walls and a roof. Most buildings also include plumbing, wiring, and heating and air conditioning equipment. A high-rise building usually has elevators and may have specially designed platforms, hoists, and tracks used by window washers. Such equipment is also considered part of the building. Property that is permanently attached to the structure, such as wall-to-wall carpeting, built-in appliances, or paneling, also generally is considered part of the building.

Personal Property

All property that is not real property is personal property. Examples of personal property include vehicles, merchandise, furniture, tools, clothing, and oil that is transported through an underground pipeline. For insurance purposes, it is useful to categorize personal property into these classifications:

- Contents
- Property in transit
- Property in the possession of others
- Floating property

Contents

Contents
Personal property that is usually contained in a building or other structure.

Personal property contained in buildings is called **contents**. The contents of a commercial building might include these items:

- Furniture, such as the desks in an office
- Machinery and equipment, such as cash registers
- Stock, such as raw materials and completed products in inventory

Although most insurance policies use the term "personal property" to refer to the contents of a building, many insurance practitioners and policyholders use the term "contents" as a matter of convenience and common practice.

Property insurance policies typically refer to personal property, rather than contents, because the property often is covered even when it is not literally contained in the building. When the contents of a commercial building are involved, policies generally use the term "business personal property."

Property in Transit

Most businesses ship property (such as merchandise) to others or receive property (such as raw materials or supplies) from others. Property in transit may be transported by truck, railcar, airplane, watercraft, or even by bicycle or on foot. A shipment may be sent to a client's office a few blocks away, to a buyer on the other side of the world, or anywhere in between. Property in transit may be transported on the owner's own vehicles or by a transportation company. The property may be in transit for a few minutes or for several months. Because of all these variables, most insurance policies covering buildings and contents exclude property in transit. A firm that wishes to insure its property in transit must usually purchase separate cargo insurance.

Property in the Possession of Others

In many situations, an organization may place its property in the temporary possession of others for processing, cleaning, repair, adjustment, storage, exhibition, or sale. Because the probability of loss at the temporary location could differ greatly from the probability of loss at the owner's location, building and contents insurance policies usually provide only a nominal amount of insurance for property at other locations.

Like property in transit, property in the possession of others can be insured for its full value under specialized policies designed for that purpose.

Floating Property

Many businesses own property that normally is situated at ever-changing work sites or in transit between work sites. Examples of this kind of property include a wedding photographer's cameras and a building contractor's tools and mobile equipment. Such property is often referred to as "floating property" because it does not remain at a single location for a sustained period. Insurance for such property is available under specialized inland marine policies called "floaters."

Perils and Hazards

The terms "peril" and "hazard" are often confused.

A peril is a cause of loss. Fire, theft, and flood are examples of perils that cause property losses. (Many property insurance policies use the term "cause of loss" instead of "peril.")

A hazard is anything that increases the likelihood of a loss or the possible severity of a loss. These are examples of hazards:

- Careless smoking practices are a fire hazard because they increase the likelihood of a fire.
- Paint cans and oily rags are fire hazards because they enable a fire to spread and cause severe damage.
- Keeping large amounts of money in a cash register overnight is a theft hazard affecting both the likelihood of loss and the severity of loss. This practice would attract thieves if they became aware of it. The amount that would be stolen—the severity of the loss—is also affected by the amount of cash in the register.

Causes of Loss to Property

The potential causes of loss to property are another important aspect of property loss exposures. A cause of loss adversely affects property and leaves it in an altered state. For example, a fire can reduce a building to a heap of rubble. Vandalism can damage a building or its contents. Some causes of loss do not alter the property itself but do affect a person's ability to possess or use the property. For example, property lost or stolen may still be used, but not by its rightful owner.

Buildings and personal property are subject to many potential causes of loss. Some of the most significant perils include fire, theft, windstorm, flood, earthquake, terrorism, and war. For most insureds, fire is the peril that poses the greatest risk of a large or even total property loss. Hurricanes and tornadoes are both examples of windstorms, although less violent windstorms also can cause property damage. Windstorms pose a catastrophic exposure for insurers and insureds in areas exposed to hurricanes. For instance, in 2005, Hurricane Katrina caused more than $34 billion in damage, while four hurricanes that struck Florida and other areas of the United States caused $22 billion in damage in 2004. Similarly, flood, earthquake, terrorism, and war pose catastrophic exposures. For example, estimates of damage from 2007 flooding in the United Kingdom exceeded $6 billion, and insured losses at the World Trade Center from the terrorist attacks of September 11, 2001, are estimated to exceed $30 billion.

Financial Consequences of Property Losses

Financial consequences are the third and final important aspect of property loss exposures. The adverse financial consequences of a property loss may include a reduction in the value of the property, lost income, and/or extra expenses.

Property Value Reduction

When a property loss occurs, the property's value is reduced. This reduction in value can be measured in different ways. Property that must be replaced has no remaining worth, unless some salvageable items can be sold. If the property can be repaired or restored, the reduction in value can be measured by the cost of the repair or restoration. For example, if a fence worth $7,000 is damaged by a falling tree and the fence owner has to pay $2,000 to have the damage repaired, the fence owner has incurred a partial loss that reduces the value of the fence by $2,000.

Lost Income

A business may lose income as a result of a property loss. When property is damaged, income might be lost because the property cannot be used until it is repaired, restored, or replaced. For example, when a business suffers a serious fire, it might have to close until repairs to the building are made and personal property is replaced. The resulting loss of income occurs over time.

As another example, the owner of a rental property faces rental income loss if the property is damaged and temporarily unavailable for rent. The owner would probably continue to incur some expenses, such as mortgage payments and taxes, but would not receive the rent that helped pay those expenses.

Determining the amount of business income that might be lost because of a property loss requires estimating an organization's future level of activity and performing a "what if" analysis that asks, "What if the business could not operate for six months because it would take six months to rebuild after a fire? How much income would be lost?"

Extra Expenses

For a business to determine the extent of a property loss exposure, it must consider the extra expenses that the loss of the property would require.

When property is damaged, the property itself declines in value, and the owner or other affected party suffers a corresponding loss. In addition, the owner or other user of that property might incur extra expenses in acquiring a temporary substitute or in temporarily maintaining the damaged property in a usable condition. Consider these examples:

- When a store's premises are damaged, the owners might have to rent temporary space at considerably greater expense than their normal rent.
- When a newspaper company's printing presses are damaged, the company might spend extra money to print the newspaper on another newspaper company's presses.
- When a bank building is damaged, the bank might hire additional guards until the building can be made secure.

COMMERCIAL PROPERTY INSURANCE COVERAGE

To make sure that their business can survive accidental property loss, one step that prudent business owners can take is to identify their property loss exposures and insure themselves against the financial consequences of damage from fire and other causes. Such preparation includes identifying the various items of property that could be lost or damaged and determining what could occur to cause loss or damage.

Business owners should determine whether the commercial property insurance they've purchased will restore their business's financial condition to its pre-loss state in the event of a significant loss. To do so, they can familiarize themselves with the provisions of their property insurance policies regarding these elements:

- Covered property
- Covered locations
- Covered causes of loss
- Covered financial consequences, such as loss of business income

Property insurance policy provisions must specify exactly which property loss exposures they cover—that is, the types and locations of property covered and the covered causes of loss.

Covered Property

A property insurance policy specifies the property that it covers by identifying it with a broad description and then refining that description through a series of limitations and exclusions. The **Building and Personal Property Coverage Form (BPP)** often is used to insure buildings, the insured's personal property (referred to as "your business personal property"), and the personal property of others. The insured can buy coverage for any combination of these three categories. However, the BPP and similar commercial property forms exclude coverage for certain types of structures (such as bridges) and certain types of business personal property (such as money and securities). Moreover, the BPP and similar forms provide only very limited coverage for property away from the insured's premises. Consequently, insurers offer additional types of property coverage, such as inland marine insurance, to cover loss exposures that are excluded by the BPP and similar forms.

> **Building and Personal Property Coverage Form (BPP)**
> A commercial property coverage form that can be used to cover buildings, "your business personal property," and personal property of others.

Buildings

In commercial property insurance, a permanent structure with walls and a roof usually is called a building. Other outdoor structures, such as carports, antenna towers, and swimming pools, though not considered buildings in the traditional sense, still may be insured under building coverage. The BPP's definition of building also includes these kinds of property:

- Completed additions to covered buildings
- Fixtures (including outdoor fixtures)
- Permanently installed machinery and equipment
- Personal property owned by the insured and used to maintain or service the building or its premises (for example, fire extinguishing equipment; outdoor furniture; and equipment for refrigeration, ventilation, cooking, dishwashing, or laundering)

Building coverage's inclusion of some items of personal property allows a building owner (such as a landlord) who has no other building contents to insure to forgo purchasing separate personal property insurance. This is advantageous because, typically, the rate for building insurance is lower than the rate for personal property insurance.

"Your Business Personal Property"

The BPP and other commercial property insurance policies usually refer to the contents of buildings as "business personal property." The BPP's definition of "your business personal property" specifies that coverage for business personal property applies to such items as furniture, machinery, and equipment that are not part of the building; and to stock, which includes merchandise, raw materials, and in-process or finished goods. Generally, coverage applies only when the property is located in or on the described building or in the open (or in a vehicle) within 100 feet of the premises.

Personal Property of Others

Coverage for personal property of others is designed to protect the insured against loss or damage to the personal property of others while such property is in the custody of the insured. Such coverage is important for businesses (generally referred to as "bailees") that have customers' property in their custody, such as laundries, dry cleaners, appliance repair shops, and furniture upholstery shops. The BPP covers such property only while it is in the insured's care, custody, or control and in or on the building described in the policy declarations or within 100 feet of the described premises. Coverage applies regardless of whether the insured is legally responsible for the damage.

Property Covered by Inland Marine Policies

Inland marine insurance provides a way to cover many loss exposures that the BPP and similar forms exclude. These exposures include property in transit; property situated at the premises of others; and "floating property," such as a contractor's tools and equipment, which could be situated at several different job sites during the policy period.

Insurers prefer to insure such property separately from the BPP because it gives them the opportunity to impose insurance conditions and rates that are appropriate for the loss exposures being covered.

These are examples of property that might be insured under an inland marine coverage form:

- Goods in domestic transit
- Property of the insured in the possession of others
- Movable equipment
- Unusual property, such as a collection of antique cars
- Instrumentalities of transportation and communication such as bridges, tunnels, docks, pipelines, and radio and television towers

Covered Locations

In addition to describing covered property, a commercial property insurance policy identifies where the property is covered. This often is defined by geographical boundaries.

The identification of a covered building generally is not problematic because its location is fixed. However, determining the location of covered personal property is not always as simple. One challenge lies in describing *precisely* what is and is not covered under an insurance policy that provides building and personal property coverage. This determination can be further complicated because buildings and personal property do not necessarily remain at a fixed location. For example, portions of a building might be removed from the premises for repair or storage, furniture might be found not only inside buildings but also on outdoor patios and decks, or items usually kept in a building might be temporarily located in a car or truck.

Commercial property policies often include a supplemental additional coverage (known as a "coverage extension") that provides a certain amount of coverage, such as $10,000, for property temporarily situated at other premises. This extension, however, applies only to losses that occur in the specified policy territory, typically the United States and Canada.

Inland marine insurance policies are designed to cover personal property that moves from place to place. These are examples of policies that cover movable personal property:

- Inland marine transportation policies that cover property transported on trucks or other conveyances
- Inland marine contractors' equipment policies that cover earthmovers and other construction equipment

Policies covering floating (movable) property might have territorial limits, or might provide coverage anywhere in the world.

Covered Causes of Loss

In addition to covered property and covered locations, property policy provisions also specify the covered causes of loss. A cause of loss (peril) is the actual means by which property is damaged or destroyed. Commercial property insurance policies on buildings and personal property are available with three different degrees of coverage:

- Basic form coverage—the lowest-cost version that provides coverage for approximately a dozen named perils.
- Broad form coverage—a higher-cost version that adds several perils to those covered by basic coverage.
- Special form (open perils) coverage—the highest-cost version that covers all causes of loss that are not specifically excluded. Special form coverage covers all the perils of broad form coverage, as well as other perils.

Property insurance policies define many causes of loss in some detail. The precise definitions vary by policy.

Basic Form Coverage

The causes of loss generally included in commercial property policies that provide basic form coverage are fire; lightning; explosion; windstorm or hail; smoke; aircraft or vehicles; riot or civil commotion; vandalism; sprinkler leakage; sinkhole collapse; volcanic action; and fungus, wet rot, dry rot, and bacteria (provided as an additional limited coverage).

Broad Form Coverage

Some property insurance policies add coverage against additional causes of loss, and are commonly referred to as "broad form coverage" policies. The additional causes of loss covered under broad form coverage are: falling objects; weight of snow, ice, or sleet; water damage; and collapse caused by certain perils (provided as an additional coverage).

Covered Causes of Loss in Basic and Broad Forms

Both Forms Cover:	Broad Form Also Covers:
Fire	Falling objects
Lightning	Weight of snow, ice, or sleet
Explosion	Water damage
Windstorm or hail	Collapse caused by certain perils (provided as an additional coverage)
Smoke	
Aircraft or vehicles	
Riot or civil commotion	
Vandalism	
Sprinkler leakage	
Sinkhole collapse	
Volcanic action	
Fungus, wet rot, dry rot, and bacteria (provided as an additional limited coverage)	

Special Form (Open Perils) Coverage

"Special form coverage" or "open perils" are terms that describe the coverage provided in commercial property insurance policies covering all causes of loss that are not specifically excluded. For example, the special form includes coverage for theft of covered property, a peril not included under the basic and broad forms. Special form coverage policies were once described as "all-risk," but this term is now less commonly used because it may be misconstrued to mean that all risks of loss are covered.

Causes of Loss Often Excluded

Insurance functions most effectively when many insureds pay relatively small premiums in order to provide a fund for paying large losses incurred by relatively few insureds. Some perils that affect a large group of people at the same time generally are considered to be commercially uninsurable, because the resulting losses would be so widespread that the funds of the entire insurance business might be inadequate to pay all of the claims.

Therefore, nearly all property insurance policies exclude coverage for losses from catastrophes such as war and nuclear reaction. Insurance against losses to property from nuclear reaction is available for nuclear power plants and transporters of nuclear materials. Most property insurance policies also exclude property losses resulting from governmental action, such as governmental seizure of property.

Most policies that provide coverage on buildings and personal property at fixed locations exclude coverage for earthquake and flood losses. An earthquake can be a catastrophe that affects many different properties in the same geographic area at the same time. Also, the extent of earthquake damage partially depends on the property's type of construction. A building that is susceptible to fire damage might be less susceptible to earthquake damage, and vice versa. For these and other reasons, insurers prefer to handle earthquake coverage separately.

Though flood damage also can be catastrophic, floods are much more predictable than earthquakes. Flooding is inevitable for property in low-lying areas near rivers, creeks, or streams. Flood insurance on buildings and personal property is available through the federal government's National Flood Insurance Program. Insurers generally are not willing to provide coverage for a loss that is certain to occur, but in certain situations, private insurers do issue flood insurance that does not involve the federal program.

Inland marine policies usually provide special form coverage, often without certain exclusions, such as flood and earthquake, that are standard for BPP policies. In some instances, basic or broad form coverage may be used for inland marine policies.

Inherent vice
A quality of or condition within a particular type of property that tends to make the property destroy itself.

Latent defect
A fault or flaw in property that is not discoverable by reasonable inspection.

Property insurance policies also typically exclude loss from **inherent vice** and **latent defect**, as well as wear and tear and other "maintenance perils." Such losses generally are uninsurable because they either are certain to occur over time, or are avoidable by performing regular maintenance and care. Maintenance perils that are excluded from most policies include:

- Wear and tear
- Marring and scratching
- Rust
- Gradual seepage of water
- Damage by insects, birds, rodents, or other animals

These maintenance perils usually are not covered even in the broadest property insurance policies. Some of these excluded perils (wear and tear, marring and scratching, or rust) involve the results of ordinary use and aging rather than unexpected damage. Damage from the other perils (water seepage, insects, or rodents) is usually preventable through proper care and maintenance.

> **Inherent Vice and Latent Defect**
>
> Examples of inherent vice include perishable goods, such as meat or fruit, that will spoil or decay over time, particularly without refrigeration. Another example of inherent vice is wood, which will warp if it is subject to humidity for a prolonged period.
>
> Examples of latent defect include aluminum siding that, because of a problem with the formula used to produce the paint for the siding, begins to peel two years after installation. Roof shingles designed to last fifteen years whose chemical composition causes them to begin to deteriorate in only five years are another example of latent defect.

Business Income

Although commercial property insurance is primarily associated with coverage for the reduction in value of property (building or personal property) that has been damaged or destroyed, it also can cover other financial consequences of a property loss, including lost income and extra expenses, both of which can be covered under business income insurance.

Business income insurance covers the reduction in the organization's net income resulting from a suspension of the insured's operations because of damage by a covered cause of loss to property at the insured's location. By covering the insured's reduction in net income, business income insurance can restore the business to the financial position it would have been in had no direct loss occurred.

Extra expenses are expenses, in addition to ordinary expenses, that an organization incurs to mitigate the effects of a business interruption. Business income insurance policies commonly include coverage for extra expenses, or extra expense insurance can be purchased in a separate form. Either way, extra expense insurance covers additional expenses incurred to reduce the length of the business interruption or that enable a business to continue some operations despite damage to its property. For example, Iris, an insurance agent, might rent office space to conduct her business at a temporary location during the repairs to her office building following a fire. Iris's rental expense would be covered as an extra expense, as would any expenses beyond her normal expenses, such as the costs of installing telephone service and of notifying her customers of the temporary location.

Business income insurance
Insurance that covers the reduction in an organization's income when operations are interrupted by damage to property caused by a covered peril.

Extra expenses
Expenses, in addition to ordinary expenses, that an organization incurs to mitigate the effects of a business interruption.

SUMMARY

Three important aspects of property loss exposures are the types of property that might be exposed to loss, damage, or destruction; the causes of loss that might result in property being lost, damaged, or destroyed; and the financial consequences of a property loss. All property can be classified as real property or personal property. Real property includes land and buildings or other structures permanently attached to the land. Personal property includes contents, property in transit, property in the possession of others, and floating property. A cause of loss (peril) adversely affects property and leaves it in an altered state. The adverse financial consequences of a property loss might include a reduction in the value of the property, lost income, or extra expenses.

Commercial property insurance policies define exactly which property loss exposures they cover by specifying the types and locations of covered property and the covered causes of loss. The Building and Personal Property Coverage Form (BPP) often is used to insure buildings and other structures, the insured's business personal property, and the personal property of others. Inland marine insurance covers miscellaneous types of loss exposures that are excluded by the BPP, such as goods in domestic transit, property of the insured in the possession of others, and movable equipment. Commercial property insurance policies specify covered locations, with specific rules for locations of business personal property. A cause of loss (peril) is the actual means by which property is damaged or destroyed. Commercial property insurance policies are available with basic form coverage, broad form coverage, or special form (open perils) coverage. Business income insurance protects a business from income lost and/or extra expenses that it incurs because of a covered direct loss to its building or personal property.

Direct Your Learning

Commercial Liability Insurance

Educational Objectives

After learning the content of this chapter and completing the corresponding course guide assignment, you should be able to:

▸ Identify the common liability loss exposures of commercial insureds

▸ Identify the coverage provided by the following types of commercial liability insurance and the loss exposures each protects against:

- General liability insurance
- Business auto insurance
- Workers compensation and employers liability insurance
- Umbrella liability insurance

Outline

Commercial Liability Loss Exposures

Commercial Liability Insurance Coverages

Summary

Commercial Liability Insurance

COMMERCIAL LIABILITY LOSS EXPOSURES

Commercial liability loss exposures can arise from a business's premises, operations, products, completed work, automobiles, and employees.

To identify a commercial liability loss exposure, one must understand these:

- The elements of a liability loss exposure
- The categories of commercial liability loss exposures

Elements of a Liability Loss Exposure

Personal auto policies and homeowners policies adequately address many loss exposures that affect individuals and families. Some loss exposures, however, require additional types of insurance.

Basis for Legal Liability

Legal liability usually is based on **tort** law, or, in some cases, on **statutes**. The central concern of tort law is determining liability for injury or loss. A tort is any wrongful act other than a crime or breach of contract. The most common type of tort is **negligence**, which occurs when a party fails to exercise the degree of care that a reasonable person in a similar situation would exercise to avoid harming others.

A statute is a law enacted by a legislature. Some statutes extend, restrict, or clarify the rights of injured parties in order to ensure that they are adequately compensated for their injuries, regardless of fault. Workers compensation laws and no-fault auto laws, which give one party the right to recover from another or restrict that right of recovery, are prominent examples of such statutes.

Potential Financial Consequences

If a court finds that a person or an organization making a liability claim has sustained some definite injury or harm, it may require the legally liable party to pay damages to the injured party.

Damages are a monetary award that one party is required to pay to another as compensation for loss or injury. In addition to having to pay damages, the legally liable party might also incur costs to defend itself in court and suffer other consequences, such as loss of reputation, that have financial ramifications.

Tort
A wrongful act or omission, other than a crime or a breach of contract, for which the remedy is usually monetary damages.

Statute
A written law passed by a legislative body, at either the federal or state level.

Negligence
A tort that occurs when a person exposes others to an unreasonable risk of harm because of failure to exercise the required degree of care.

Categories of Commercial Liability Loss Exposures

Four of the most important categories of commercial liability loss exposures are premises and operations liability, products and completed operations liability, automobile liability, and workers compensation and employers liability.

Premises and Operations Liability Loss Exposure

The premises and operations liability loss exposure entails the possibility that an organization will be held liable because of bodily injury or property damage caused by either of these kinds of accidents:

- An accident occurring on premises (land, buildings, or other structures) it owns, leases, or rents
- An accident occurring away from such premises, but only if it arises out of the organization's ongoing (as opposed to completed) operations

Premises liability exposure
Exposure to liability for injury or damage due to the ownership, occupancy, or use of premises.

The **premises liability exposure** arises from ownership, occupancy, or use of property (the premises). For example, an accident that could lead to a premises liability claim against an organization might involve a visitor being injured because of dangerous conditions on the premises, such as icy walkways, uneven stairs, sharp objects, unguarded machinery, insufficient security, or a fire.

Operations liability exposure
Exposure to liability for injury or damage due to activities in addition to the ownership, occupancy, or use of premises.

The **operations liability exposure** arises from activity in addition to the occupancy of property. Although the operations could be those of any kind of business, this exposure is generally associated with manufacturers, processors, or contractors. For example, a contractor paving a road has an operations liability exposure. If a member of the public is injured as a result of negligent construction activity that occurs while the road is being paved, any resulting liability claim against the contractor is considered to have arisen from the operations liability exposure.

> **Examples of Commercial Liability Loss Exposures**
>
> Premises Liability Exposure: A customer trips on an uneven carpet in a retail store or slips on an icy pavement outside the store.
>
> Operations Liability Exposure: A member of the public is injured when a contractor doing electrical work in an office building drops a large piece of equipment.

Products and Completed Operations Liability Loss Exposure

Liability for products and liability for completed operations are so similar that they are usually handled jointly in commercial liability insurance. Nevertheless, products liability and completed operations liability each have distinguishing characteristics.

The **products liability exposure** relates to the potential legal liability of the manufacturer, distributor, or retailer to the user or consumer of a product because of injury or damage resulting from the product. The liability is based on the manufacture, distribution, or sale of an unsafe, dangerous, or defective product and the failure of the manufacturer, distributor, or retailer to meet the legal duties associated with that product.

Products liability exposure
Exposure to liability for injury or damage due to products sold or distributed by the exposed party.

Products Liability Loss Exposure—An Example
A child receives a toboggan that was purchased from a sporting goods store as a gift. The first time the child uses the toboggan, it suddenly veers off course and crashes into a tree. The child breaks several bones and requires surgery and a one-week hospital stay. The insurer would need to determine if the injury was the result of a product that was defective when it left the factory, damaged between the factory and the customer, or damaged by the customer. The customer (in this case, the child's parent) could sue both the store and the manufacturer. Both the store and the manufacturer would need products liability coverage to cover such a loss.

The **completed operations liability exposure** relates to the potential legal liability of a contractor, repairer, or other entity for losses arising from the entity's completed work. An example of completed operations liability would be a lawsuit filed against a decking construction contractor alleging injury to persons who had been standing on a backyard wooden deck when it collapsed.

Completed operations liability exposure
Exposure to liability for injury or damage due to work completed by the exposed party.

Products and Completed Operations Liability Loss Exposures
Products liability coverage pays for bodily injury or property damage that takes place away from the insured's premises and is caused by a product sold by the insured.

Completed operations liability coverage pays for bodily injury or property damage caused by work that the insured has completed, such as repair work to a customer's property.

Some activities, such as installing an accessory in customer-owned equipment, involve both a product (the accessory) and an operation (the installation). It is usually unnecessary for an insurer to decide whether a claim relates to a product or to a completed operation because both coverages are written together as part of the commercial liability coverage.

Automobile Liability Loss Exposure
Automobile liability consists of legal responsibility for bodily injury or property damage arising out of the ownership, maintenance, or use of automobiles (cars, trucks, trailers). Mobile equipment—such as forklifts, bulldozers, mobile cranes, and similar equipment—is not included in the auto liability category. The activities that create auto liability loss exposures can be classified as ownership, maintenance, and use.

Simply owning an auto can be the basis for auto liability. For example, an auto owner can be held legally liable for negligent operation of the owner's auto even when the auto is operated by a borrower using the auto for his or her own purposes. Many states have enacted statutes that make an auto owner liable for operation of the auto by any person who uses the auto with the owner's permission.

Negligent maintenance of an auto can also be the basis for auto liability. For example, negligent servicing of brakes, tires, or steering apparatus may cause a truck to collide with another vehicle.

Negligent use of an auto is the most likely way a business can incur auto liability. Whether the organization's owner or an employee is using the vehicle, the organization is generally held liable for a loss resulting from negligent use of an auto.

Workers Compensation and Employers Liability Loss Exposure

Workers compensation and employers liability are separate, but related, exposures that result from the possibility that an employee might be injured at work. Such injury can be the result of a single accident or long-term exposure to harmful conditions (occupational disease).

An employer's responsibility to pay claims under workers compensation statutes is a common example of liability imposed by statute. The term "workers compensation statutes" includes the various state workers compensation statutes as well as similar federal statutes that apply to certain types of employees, such as maritime employees. Workers compensation statutes require employers to pay certain benefits to employees who suffer an occupational injury or disease. These benefits include medical costs, lost wages, and temporary or permanent disability income.

In addition to being liable to pay statutory benefits, an employer has an employers liability exposure for tort suits as a result of occupational injury or disease to its employees in two general situations. The first situation occurs when the injured employee is covered by a workers compensation statute but the particular injury (such as intentional injury committed by the employer) is one for which the law has nevertheless permitted tort suits. The second situation occurs when the injured employee (such as a farm worker or a casual employee) is not covered by a workers compensation statute.

COMMERCIAL LIABILITY INSURANCE COVERAGES

A commercial organization may purchase commercial liability insurance coverages to cover its loss exposures.

Any organization, whether operating for-profit or not-for-profit, faces a variety of liability loss exposures that could cause the organization to fail. One way for organizations to manage liability loss exposures is to transfer the financial consequences of those exposures to an insurer by purchasing commercial liability insurance. Four common types of commercial liability insurance are general liability insurance, business auto insurance, workers compensation and employers liability insurance, and umbrella liability insurance.

General Liability Insurance

Commercial general liability (CGL) insurance is the foundation for most organizations' liability insurance programs. The most commonly used standard form for providing CGL insurance is the Commercial General Liability Coverage Form of Insurance Services Office, Inc. (ISO), an insurance advisory organization. The CGL coverage form provides three separate coverages:

- Coverage A—Bodily Injury and Property Damage Liability
- Coverage B—Personal and Advertising Injury Liability
- Coverage C—Medical Payments

Coverage A—Bodily Injury and Property Damage Liability

In Coverage A of the CGL, the insurer agrees to pay those sums that the insured becomes legally obligated to pay as damages because of bodily injury or property damage to which the insurance applies. The insurer also agrees to defend the insured against claims or suits seeking damages covered under the policy.

As defined in the CGL, bodily injury includes bodily injury, sickness, disease, or death; and property damage means physical injury to property and resulting loss of use of that property, or loss of use of property that is not physically injured.

Subject to applicable exclusions and conditions, Coverage A insures two general categories of loss exposures:

- Premises and operations liability
- Products and completed operations liability

The premises and operations liability loss exposure entails the possibility that an organization will be held liable because of bodily injury or property damage caused either by an accident occurring on premises (land, buildings, or other structures) owned, leased, or rented by the organization, or caused by an accident occurring away from such premises, but only if it arises out of the organization's ongoing (as opposed to completed) operations.

Personal and advertising injury
Injury that is covered by Coverage B of the CGL and includes injury resulting from numerous offenses, such as false detention, malicious prosecution, wrongful eviction, slander, libel, use of another's advertising idea, and copyright infringement.

Libel
A written or printed untrue statement that damages a person's reputation.

Slander
A defamatory statement expressed by speech.

False arrest
The seizure or forcible restraint of a person without legal authority.

Business Auto Coverage Form
A coverage form, filed by ISO, that covers liability arising out of the ownership, maintenance, or use of autos and physical damage to autos owned, leased, or hired by the named insured.

The products and completed operations liability loss exposure entails the possibility that an organization will be held liable because of bodily injury or property damage arising out of products sold or distributed by the insured or arising out of operations that the insured has completed or abandoned.

Coverage B—Personal and Advertising Injury Liability

In Coverage B of the CGL, the insurer agrees to pay those sums that the insured becomes legally obligated to pay as damages because of **personal and advertising injury** to which the insurance applies. The insurer also agrees to defend the insured against claims or suits seeking damages covered under the policy.

As defined in the CGL, personal and advertising injury means injury arising out of any of several specified offenses (torts) that could be committed in the course of the insured's operations or advertising activities. Examples of such offenses are **libel, slander, false arrest**, and use of another's advertising idea. In this definition, the word "injury" is not defined by the policy but takes its usual broad meaning. It therefore includes, for example, injury to financial condition, injury to reputation, and psychological injury. The policy states that personal and advertising injury even includes bodily injury that results from one of the specified offenses, such as bodily injury resulting from false arrest.

Coverage C—Medical Payments

In Coverage C of the CGL, the insurer agrees to pay medical expenses for bodily injury caused by an accident occurring on the insured's premises. The insurer also agrees to pay medical expenses for bodily injury caused by an accident that occurs away from the insured's premises (for example, at a job site where the insured is working) if the accident results from the named insured's operations.

Medical payments coverage pays regardless of whether the insured is legally liable. Therefore, it is not technically liability insurance, even though it is commonly included in liability insurance policies.

The purpose of medical payments coverage is to provide a modest amount of insurance for settling minor injury cases without requiring a determination of liability. In that sense, the coverage provides a means of making prompt settlements, satisfying potential liability claimants, and avoiding possibly larger liability claims.

Business Auto Insurance

CGL insurance policies exclude most auto liability exposures. Consequently, an organization that uses autos also needs liability insurance for the ownership, maintenance, and use of those autos. The **Business Auto Coverage Form**, another ISO standard form, is widely used to meet the auto liability insurance needs of most types of organizations.

In the Business Auto Coverage Form, the insurer agrees to pay all sums the insured legally must pay as damages because of bodily injury or property damage to which the insurance applies caused by an accident and resulting from the ownership, maintenance, or use of a covered auto. The insurer also agrees to defend the insured against any claim or suit alleging damages that would be covered under the policy.

"Ownership, maintenance, or use" of an auto includes virtually any activity involving a covered auto for which an insured might be held liable, including these kinds of liability:

- Liability as an owner of the auto
- Liability for injury resulting from faulty maintenance of the auto
- Liability for use or operation of the auto by the insured organization

The insured indicates the categories of autos it wishes the policy to cover by selecting numerical symbols in the policy. Covered autos for liability insurance can include autos owned, leased, or hired by the named insured, as well as autos that the insured does not own, lease, or hire but that are used on the insured's behalf (such as an employee using his or her own auto on the insured's business).

Workers Compensation and Employers Liability Insurance

Almost all employers purchase **workers compensation and employers liability insurance** to cover these loss exposures:

- The insured's obligation to pay benefits required by a **workers compensation statute**
- The insured's liability to pay damages because of injury to the insured's employees as a result of a claim or suit based on legal grounds other than a workers compensation statute

Workers compensation statutes exist in all states and other jurisdictions of the United States, every Canadian province, and some other nations. These laws, in return for removing the right of injured employees to sue their employers for occupational injury, obligate employers to compensate injured employees regardless of whether their injuries resulted from the employer's negligence. The workers compensation system guarantees injured workers prompt payment while reducing costs and court workloads that arise from litigation. Workers compensation statutes apply to almost all types of private employment. Very large employers can self-insure in some instances, but most employers buy workers compensation insurance that will pay injured workers the benefits required by law.

Workers compensation and employers liability insurance
Insurance that covers (1) benefits an employer is obligated to pay under workers compensation laws and (2) employee injury claims made against the employer that are not covered by workers compensation laws.

Workers compensation statute
A statute that obligates employers, regardless of fault, to pay specified medical, disability, rehabilitation, and death benefits for their employees' job-related injuries and diseases.

In most of the U.S., workers compensation and employers liability insurance is provided under a standard form known as the Workers Compensation and Employers Liability Insurance Policy (WC&EL policy) developed by the National Council on Compensation Insurance (NCCI), an insurance advisory organization. The WC&EL policy provides its two basic coverages in these coverage sections:

- Part 1—Workers Compensation Insurance
- Part 2—Employers Liability Insurance

Part 1—Workers Compensation Insurance

In Part 1—Workers Compensation Insurance, the insurer agrees to pay promptly when due the benefits required of the insured by the workers compensation law of any state listed in the policy's Information Page. These are the benefits usually required by workers compensation laws:

- Unlimited medical expense benefits for a covered injury or disease
- Disability income benefits, which compensate an injured employee for wage loss due to a covered injury or disease
- Rehabilitation benefits, which include expenses for complete medical rehabilitation (and sometimes vocational rehabilitation) following a covered injury or disease
- Death benefits, which include a flat amount for burial expenses as well as partial replacement of the worker's former weekly wage

Part 2—Employers Liability Insurance

In Part 2—Employers Liability Insurance, the insurer agrees to pay all sums the insured legally must pay as damages because of bodily injury to the insured's employees, provided the bodily injury is covered by the Employers Liability Insurance section. Because employers liability insurance excludes any obligation imposed by a workers compensation or similar law, most occupational injuries and illnesses are covered under Part 1—Workers Compensation Insurance. An example of a claim that could be covered under employers liability insurance is a bodily injury claim made by an employee whose occupation (such as farm work) is not covered by the applicable workers compensation law.

Umbrella Liability Insurance

An umbrella liability policy provides limits of insurance that apply in addition to the limits of the insured's primary liability policies, including CGL, business auto, employers liability, and other liability policies. Umbrella liability coverage is also referred to as "excess" coverage because it applies in excess of the primary coverages.

Insureds need umbrella or excess liability coverage because the maximum loss for most liability exposures cannot easily be estimated. Awards to injured persons can, in some cases, reach extremely high totals. For example, hundreds of verdicts in excess of $1 million are made each year in the U.S. Although most organizations are not likely to experience such losses, the possibility of a large liability loss exists for virtually any business.

Umbrella liability coverage becomes applicable when the amount of damages for which the insured is liable exceeds the limit of an underlying policy. Umbrella policies may also cover, on a primary basis, some claims that are not covered at all by the underlying policy or policies. Such coverage is often referred to as "drop-down coverage." Each insurer writing umbrella liability policies has its own requirements for the types and amounts of underlying insurance that the insured must have.

SUMMARY

A liability loss exposure entails the possibility of one party becoming legally liable for injury or harm to another party. The elements of a liability loss exposure include the basis for legal liability (torts or statutes) and the potential financial consequences of liability loss exposures (damages, defense costs, and damage to reputation). Four common categories of commercial liability loss exposures are premises and operations liability, products and completed operations liability, automobile liability, and workers compensation and employers liability.

Four common types of commercial liability insurance are general liability insurance, business auto insurance, workers compensation and employers liability insurance, and umbrella liability insurance. Organizations commonly purchase commercial general liability insurance to cover premises, operations, products, and completed operations loss exposures. A business using automobiles needs liability insurance that covers the ownership, maintenance, and use of those autos. Most employers buy workers compensation and employers liability insurance, which will pay injured workers the benefits required by workers compensation laws and cover the insured employer in cases where the law permits employees to sue their employers for occupational injury or disease. An umbrella liability policy provides excess coverage over one or more primary liability policies and may also cover, on a primary basis, some claims that are not covered at all by the underlying policies.

Direct Your Learning

Chapter 10

Premium Determination

Educational Objectives

After learning the content of this chapter and completing the corresponding course guide assignment, you should be able to:

▸ Explain how an insurance premium is determined.

▸ Summarize how insurance rates are developed.

▸ Identify the types of rate(s) and the rating basis used for the following kinds of insurance:
- Personal auto insurance
- Homeowners insurance
- Commercial property insurance
- Inland marine insurance
- Commercial general liability insurance
- Business auto insurance
- Workers compensation insurance

▸ Identify the types of rating plans that are used in determining insurance premiums.

Outline

How an Insurance Premium Is Determined

Developing Insurance Rates

Types of Rates and Rating Basis

Types of Rating Plans

Summary

Premium Determination

HOW AN INSURANCE PREMIUM IS DETERMINED

Understanding how an insurance premium is determined first requires defining what an insurance premium is and the insurance **rates** and exposure units that are used in determining the insurance premium. Calculating an insurance premium involves multiplying rate times the number of exposure units. Other factors also affect insurance premium determination.

An insurance premium is a periodic payment by the insured to the insurer in exchange for insurance coverage. "Periodic" means that the payment must be made at certain time intervals. Each premium payment buys insurance protection for a particular time period, such as one year.

Insurance premiums provide the funds with which an insurer pays claims. Insurance premiums also pay the insurer's expenses and provide funds for the insurer's investments.

Insurers' earnings on their investments supplement the income they receive from insurance premiums. To some extent, investment income can reduce the amount insurers would otherwise have to charge as premiums. If an insurer is to succeed in the long run, its premium income and its investment income, together, must be at least adequate to pay claims and expenses—preferably, with some money left for profits and contingencies.

Rate
The price per exposure unit for insurance coverage.

Determining an Insurance Premium

An insurance premium is calculated by multiplying the insurance rate times the number of exposure units.

Insurance Rates

Insurance rates are developed through insurance rating systems. These rating systems rely on statistical analysis of past losses to determine what rates insurers should charge. Insurers add their allowance for their expenses, profits, and contingencies to arrive at the rate that they charge insureds for a particular loss exposure. These rates typically are then quoted per some dollar amount of insurance coverage. For example, in the case of homeowners insurance, the rate is usually quoted as per $1,000 of insurance coverage.

Some lines of insurance are **class rated** by grouping insureds with similar characteristics into the same class to capture potential loss frequency and severity of the group. When an insured cannot be readily assigned to a class, the insured loss exposure is rated individually.

Class rated
A type of insurance rate that applies to all insureds in the same rating category or rating class.

Exposure Units

The fundamental measures of the loss exposures used in insurance rating are referred to as exposure units. Insurers can choose among various measures to use as exposure units. The exposure units selected for rating each insurance coverage should bear a relationship to the size of the exposures. The exposure units should be large enough to be practical yet small enough to be combined to reflect the size of a variety of losses. To be more specific, the number of exposure units should be a fair measure of expected loss frequency and severity. As the number of exposure units increases, the potential number of losses or the amount to be paid for each loss should increase.

The choice of exposure units should reflect four desirable characteristics.

> **Four Desirable Characteristics of Exposure Units**
>
> Ideally, a standard exposure unit should reflect these four characteristics:
>
> - Reflect the exposures—For example, in homeowners insurance, the exposure unit is per $1,000 of a home's value.
> - Be readily measurable—For example, a home's value can be determined through comparable sales, or by the use of a construction cost index.
> - Be inflation sensitive—For example, home values rise with inflation.
> - Be reasonably simple—For example, many people can relate to home values.

In homeowners insurance, exposure units may be expressed as $1,000 of exposure. In the case of a home insured for $400,000, the number of exposure units is 400. In the case of a home insured for $200,000, the number of exposure units is 200.

Calculation of Premium (Rate x Exposure Units)

After the insurance rates and number of insurance units are known, calculating the insurance premium involves a relatively simple mathematical formula. This type of calculation is similar to that used in pricing many products that consumers purchase.

Consider the pricing structure at a produce stand. For example, assume two peaches are sold at the price (or rate) of $0.40 per peach. The cost is determined by multiplying the rate per peach times the number of peaches:

$$\text{Rate per unit} \times \text{Number of units} = \text{Price}.$$
$$\$0.40 \text{ per peach} \times 2 \text{ peaches} = \$0.80.$$

The same formula is used if five pounds of peaches are sold at the produce stand at a price of $0.98 per pound:

Rate per unit × Number of units = Price.
$0.98 per pound × 5 pounds = $4.90.

In both examples, the total cost is composed of a rate ($0.40 or $0.98) for some standard unit of purchase (peach or pound) multiplied by the number of units (two peaches and five pounds, respectively). The choice of standard units is a matter of convenience. For instance, peaches might be priced "per peach" or "by the pound"; gasoline in the United States is usually priced by the gallon, but in many other countries it is priced by the liter.

Underwriters calculating insurance premiums follow essentially the same process in determining premiums as in calculating the price of commodities. Based on rates provided by the insurance rating system and published in rating manuals, the final price of insurance (the premium) is determined by multiplying the rate per unit times the number of exposure units:

Rate per unit × Number of exposure units = Premium.

The formula is the same as before, except that in this example the word "premium" is substituted for the word "price." For example, if the insurance rating system shows a rate of $900 per auto to provide collision coverage for one year, this rate is multiplied by the number of autos to arrive at the annual premium. Consider a company with five autos to insure—the computation would be simple:

Rate per unit × Number of exposure units = Premium.
$900 per auto × 5 autos = $4,500.

Many insurance rating units are expressed in dollar amounts, such as "$100 of insured value" or "$1,000 of payroll." Suppose a building and contents policy has a rate of $0.70 per $100 of building insurance and a building is being insured for $200,000:

Building ÷ Unit size = Number of units.
$200,000 ÷ $100 = 2,000 units.
Rate per unit × Number of units = Premium.
$0.70 × 2,000 = $1,400.

Other Factors Affecting Premium Determination

Although a major part of establishing premiums is calculating rate times exposure units, other factors can affect premium determination.

The premium charged for an insurance policy should be commensurate with the exposure. That is, there should be a close relationship between the premium charged and the risk assumed by the insurer.

Insurers are not the only ones concerned about whether premiums properly reflect exposures. Insurance buyers also compare the cost of insurance with the potential losses the insurance would cover. They tend to not purchase insurance from insurers whose premiums seem too high. Insureds tend to buy insurance from the insurer with the lowest premiums. Thus, insurers generally will sell more insurance if they offer lower premiums. However, premium levels can be reduced only so far before underwriting losses result.

Ideally, insurance premiums encourage insureds to practice loss control, a risk management technique that attempts to decrease the frequency or severity of losses. Basically, this means that an insured that exercises sound loss control should pay less for insurance than one that does not.

Additionally, insurer-specific factors affect premium determination.

DEVELOPING INSURANCE RATES

Insurance rates, the basic price of insurance for each unit of exposure, are developed through insurance rating systems established by insurers and independent insurance advisory organizations. Typically, insurance rating systems are primarily based on insurers' loss costs. Insurance rating systems help to establish rates by also using either class or individual rating methodologies to analyze and categorize insureds. As part of insurance rating systems, insurers add an allowance for expenses and profits in determining the final rate for a particular loss exposure. The final premium, which is the insured's price for insurance coverage, is then determined by multiplying the final rate by the number of exposure units.

Insurance Advisory Organizations

Insurance advisory organizations work with insurers in developing insurance rating systems. **Insurance advisory organizations** are independent organizations that supply a variety of data services to the insurance industry. The largest insurance advisory organization is Insurance Services Office (ISO), which provides analytical and decision-support products and services to the property-casualty industry. The National Council on Compensation Insurance (NCCI) is an insurance advisory organization that manages a database of workers compensation insurance information, analyzes industry trends,

Insurance advisory organization
An independent organization that works with and on behalf of insurers that purchase or subscribe to its services.

Other Factors Affecting Premium Determination

Factor	Explanation of Factor	Effect on Premium
Marketing System	A direct marketing system has different costs than an agency marketing system.	A costly marketing system will require larger premiums for insureds.
Underwriting Standards	Strict underwriting standards require the insurer to be more selective in the risks to be insured. Lax underwriting standards allow the insurer to be less selective in the risks to be insured.	Insurer can charge lower premiums for the pool of better-than-average risks insured. Insurer must charge higher premiums for the greater-than-average risks insured.
Insurance Company Ownership	Both stock and mutual insurance companies desire profits for stockholders and policyholders, respectively.	Insurance companies must charge insureds adequate premiums to cover losses, expenses, and a profit.
Services	The more expensive the services provided,... (Example: loss control services)	... the more expensive the insurance premium.
Coverage	Generally, the more causes of loss covered, the greater the expense to insurers.	If more causes of loss are covered, the premium will increase.
Investment Income	Insurer reserves are invested.	Insurer investment results affect premiums charged.
Cash Flow Considerations	Insurance premiums paid by installment restrict cash flow.	The level of interest charges on installment payments will affect premiums.

prepares workers compensation rate recommendations, and assists in pricing legislation. Many other insurance advisory organizations operate in the United States.

Insurance Rating Systems

Insurance advisory organizations help to develop insurance rating systems by collecting reliable loss data that insurers use in establishing their rates and premiums. Insurance advisory organizations continually collect loss information from many insurers. For example, to assist insurers in determining what rate to charge for automobile insurance during a certain time period, insurance advisory organizations may gather data on insurers' loss costs for automobile accidents involving certain types of vehicles during a particular year.

Loss data from insurers are combined as a part of insurance rating systems. Combining these data makes the information more reliable because loss prediction is most accurate when it is based on the actual losses of a large number of exposure units.

Insurance advisory organizations then analyze the loss data to determine the average loss costs per exposure unit used in class rating.

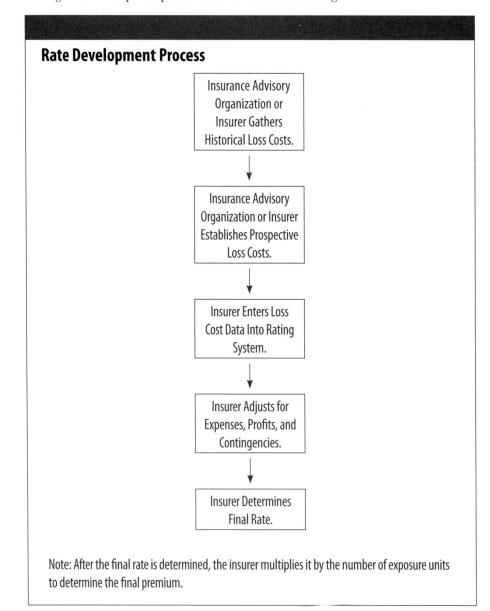

Rate Development Process

- Insurance Advisory Organization or Insurer Gathers Historical Loss Costs.
- Insurance Advisory Organization or Insurer Establishes Prospective Loss Costs.
- Insurer Enters Loss Cost Data Into Rating System.
- Insurer Adjusts for Expenses, Profits, and Contingencies.
- Insurer Determines Final Rate.

Note: After the final rate is determined, the insurer multiplies it by the number of exposure units to determine the final premium.

Loss Costs

Loss data reflect historical **loss costs**, which involve costs that occurred in the past. Insurers often adjust data on historical loss costs to anticipate losses that can be expected in the future as a result of inflation or other measurable trends. These expected future losses are called prospective loss costs. **Prospective loss costs** indicate the amount of money an insurer can expect to need to pay for future claims for each exposure unit. Of course, it is not enough for insurers to collect money only to pay claims. An insurer must also cover its expenses and allow for profits and contingencies.

Each insurer determines how much to add to prospective loss costs to arrive at the final rate it will charge. The result is that each insurer uses loss cost information to develop its own set of rates per exposure unit. These rates reflect both prospective loss costs and the insurer's expenses and are published in the insurer's rating manual or stored in the insurer's rating system. These rates are also filed with the state insurance department where required. In many cases, the state insurance department might also reject, modify, or approve the rates that will be used.

Loss costs
The portion of the rate that covers projected claim payments and loss adjusting expenses.

Prospective loss costs
Loss data modified by loss development, trending, and credibility processes, but without considerations for profit and expenses.

Class Rating

Insurers develop loss costs for many different lines (or types) of business and many different groups or classes of insureds within those lines. Many kinds of insurance are class rated. That is, a classification and rating system groups together all insureds with similar characteristics into the same rating class. All members of the class are charged the same rate for insurance, although their premiums will be different if they have different numbers of exposure units. (For example, a homeowner with a $400,000 home will pay more for homeowners insurance than a homeowner with a $200,000 home.)

The basic idea of an insurance classification and rating system is that insureds with similar characteristics have similar potential loss frequency and severity. Even though wide variation in actual losses may occur from one insured to the next, aggregate losses among all members of the class should be predictably different from the losses of all members of another class who have different characteristics. For example, an employer will pay more for workers compensation insurance for a construction worker than for a clerical worker because construction workers as a class are more likely to become injured or disabled on the job than clerical workers as a class.

While no two risks are identical, grouping them together enables an insurer to take advantage of pooling. The groupings or classes need to be big enough so that the law of large numbers is useful. (The law of large numbers is a mathematical principle stating that as the number of similar but independent exposure units increases, the relative accuracy of predictions about future outcomes, or losses, also increases.) But the groupings or classes also need to be small enough so that each member of the class is somewhat similar. That is, they must have enough characteristics similar to those of other members in the group (related to frequency and severity of loss) to be grouped together.

Individual Rating

Individual rate
A type of insurance rate that reflects the unique characteristics of an insured or the insured's property.

When insureds cannot be readily assigned to the same class, the insured loss exposure is rated individually. An **individual rate** would be developed for fire insurance on a large, unique factory building. The specific building is inspected by an underwriting professional using a point system that adds or subtracts points for such things as type of construction (masonry, wood, and so on), number and type of fire extinguishers, nature of the occupancy, capabilities of the local fire department, as well as the supply of water available at nearby hydrants. The number of points determines an insurance rate for that particular building. The rate is published so that producers, underwriters, raters, and other interested parties have access to it. The published rate is applied "per $100 of insurance" to determine the premium for fire insurance.

Judgment rating
Rating used by underwriters to rate one-of-a-kind risks.

Sometimes it is necessary to insure an exposure for which there is no established premium-determining system. In such cases, the underwriter has to rely heavily on his or her judgment, a practice that is referred to as judgment rating. **Judgment rating** is a type of individual rating. Judgment rating does not mean that an underwriter arbitrarily sets a rate for a particular exposure. The underwriter usually has experience with insurance covering comparable exposures. This experience gives the underwriter a confident sense as to what premium amount would be appropriate. For example, successful experience in insuring cross-country rail shipments of coal and iron ore might help an underwriter to decide the premium to charge for insuring the shipment of some other bulk cargo.

Final Rate and Premium Determination

Final rate
The price per exposure unit determined by adjusting the prospective loss costs for expenses, profits, and contingencies.

Final rates result from prospective loss costs that move through the rating system and become adjusted for expenses, profits, and contingencies. Insurance rating systems assist insurers in determining rates based on past and expected future losses. The rating systems also account for other factors that affect insurers' final rate determination.

To conduct business, insurers not only pay loss costs but also pay other expenses, such as underwriting and loss adjustment expenses, and plan for profits and contingencies. To set the final rates that they charge insureds for particular loss exposures, individual insurers therefore add an allowance for factors such as expenses, profits, and contingencies to the basic insurance rates developed through insurance rating systems.

After the final rate has been calculated, it is multiplied by the number of exposure units to become the final insurance premium.

TYPES OF RATES AND RATING BASIS

To determine insurance premiums, insurers use various types of rates and a rating basis for different kinds of insurance.

Insurers use class, individual, or judgment types of rates to analyze and categorize insureds in determining insurance premiums for different kinds of insurance, such as personal auto insurance, homeowners insurance, commercial property insurance, inland marine insurance, commercial general liability insurance, business auto insurance, and workers compensation insurance. Within each kind of insurance, insurers also use a rating basis to determine premiums. The rating basis is a set of relevant characteristics used to define classes in rating or as factors in individual rating.

> **Types of Rates**
>
> Class rates, individual rates, and judgment rates are the major types of rates used with different kinds of insurance.
>
> With class rating, the insureds must share enough characteristics with each other (related to frequency and severity of loss) to be grouped together. For example, in personal auto insurance, the insureds may be grouped by type of auto, by where a vehicle is kept and operated, by policy limit, or by vehicle usage.
>
> Individual rating is the approach taken in developing a commercial property insurance rate on a large, unique factory building by using a point system to add or subtract from standard rates.
>
> A judgment rate is used by an insurer when a loss exposure is so unique that the insurer has no established system by which to determine a premium. For example, judgment rating is often used for the shipment of bulk commodities by rail or sea because of variations in the commodities' characteristics and in shipping conditions.

The types of rates and the rating basis vary with each kind of insurance.

Type of Rate and Examples of Rating Basis for Different Kinds of Insurance

Kind of Insurance	Type of Rate	Examples of Rating Basis
Personal auto insurance	Class	Per auto, rating territory, policy limit, vehicle type, driver experience, vehicle usage
Homeowners insurance	Class	Dwelling value, territory, type of construction
Commercial property insurance	Class or individual	Total value, property type or class, territory
Inland marine insurance	Class or judgment	Total value, property type or class, territory
Commercial general liability insurance	Class or judgment	Payroll, gross sales, area, admissions, total cost, units
Business auto insurance	Class	Per auto, territory, type of vehicle (gross vehicle weight), type of business operation, radius of vehicle operation
Workers compensation insurance	Class	Payroll (remuneration)

Personal Auto Insurance

Personal auto insurance is designed for individuals and families who own private passenger autos, pickups, and vans. Personal auto insurance is class rated, and its rating systems often have a large number of classes. Some insurers may use more than 200 different rating classes within each geographical rating territory.

Because the United States has hundreds of rating territories, actual rating classes number well into the thousands. A system with so many different classes would not provide workable groupings for a kind of insurance with relatively few insureds (because so few insureds would be in each class). However, the more than 200 million licensed drivers in the United States provide enough exposure units to enable insurers' use of highly refined classes.

The rating basis varies among insurers. In each case, the purpose is to place insureds into groups, with the members of each group having similar loss exposures.

Personal Auto Insurance Rating Basis

These are some examples of a rating basis that can be used in personal auto insurance:

- Insurance score—based on the driver's credit history
- Driver's age, gender, and marital status
- Driver's occupation and education
- Tickets the driver has received during the past three years for traffic violations (five years for some serious violations)
- Accidents the driver has had during the past three years
- Whether any drivers have been licensed for fewer than three years
- Whether youthful drivers have had driver training
- Whether youthful drivers are good students
- Territory where the auto is garaged
- Auto's age (for physical damage insurance)
- Auto's cost when new
- Auto's safety features
- Whether the auto is used for pleasure, for commuting to work, in business, or on a farm
- Distance the auto travels to the driver's workplace
- Whether the auto is standard, high performance, or a sports car
- Whether the policy covers a single auto or more than one auto (in which case a discount might apply)

Avoiding traffic violations and accidents is not only good loss control but also leads to lower insurance premiums. Drivers who have had at-fault accidents or have been convicted of serious traffic violations pay a substantially higher premium than those with a good driving record.

Data are collected on the accident experience of specific makes and models of cars. Predictions can be made that certain types of cars are more likely to be stolen, more likely to sustain serious damage in an accident, or more likely to have injured occupants than are others. Some insurers' rating basis reflects these damageability and susceptibility factors.

Homeowners Insurance

Homeowners insurance covers most of the property and liability loss exposures that arise out of residential ownership and occupancy, as well as property and liability loss exposures that individuals and families may have while they are away from their residences. Like auto insurance, homeowners insurance is class rated. There are millions of homes in the United States, and a number of classifications have been developed, each of which include a large number of similar homes. Most states are divided into rating territories, reflecting differences in crime and vandalism claims or exposures to windstorm, hail, or other climatic conditions. These are the primary factors included in the rating basis for homeowners insurance:

- Construction type—generally frame or brick, because wood frame houses burn more readily and therefore have higher premiums than solid brick houses
- Protection class—a rating of the local fire department's capabilities and the availability of fire hydrants and other water supply sources

Various factors in addition to construction type and protection class are included in the rating basis.

> **Homeowners Insurance Rating Basis**
>
> These are some examples of a rating basis that can be used in homeowners insurance:
>
> - Assessed value of home (accounts for inflation and comparable home sales)
> - Construction type (brick or frame, etc.)
> - Protection class (fire department capability and fire hydrant availability)
> - Claims history (frequency and severity)
> - Insurance score (based on individuals' credit history)
> - Home maintenance (might include discounts for security locks, fire alarms, and security systems)
> - Location or territory (duplex or single home and distance between homes, etc.)

The typical home seldom has an insurable loss, and most homes therefore have no loss history. However, some insurers' discounts for alarm systems and other safety devices attempt to identify and reward homeowners with reduced loss potential by charging them a reduced premium.

Commercial Property Insurance

Commercial property insurance covers not only a building but also its contents. Commercial building and contents insurance can be class rated or individually rated, depending on the building. Both class rates and individual rates are stated as rates per $100 of insurance.

Some commercial buildings and their contents are of a type that has a large number of similar exposure units, such as typical gasoline stations and mini-markets. A large number of these gas stations and mini-markets can be found in every state, all with essentially the same physical characteristics. Therefore, these exposures are class rated.

Other commercial buildings are unique and thus individually rated. One-of-a-kind buildings cannot be grouped with other buildings, so it is necessary to develop commercial property insurance rates based on their own individual characteristics. Insurers examine such buildings to establish an insurance rate for each particular building. Separate rates are determined for each building and its contents. In a multiple-occupancy building, different rates for contents might be determined for each tenant.

Commercial property insurers consider a building's construction, occupancy, protection, and exposures (which can be remembered using the acronym COPE) in establishing the rating basis.

> **Commercial Property Insurance Rating Basis**
>
> Commercial property insurers have adopted the acronym of COPE (Construction, Occupancy, Protection, and External Exposures) to quickly identify loss exposures and to identify characteristics that serve as a rating basis for commercial property insurance.
>
> **Construction**
> - Building construction type (Frame, joisted masonry, noncombustible, masonry noncombustible, modified fire-resistive, fire-resistive, etc.)
> - Construction materials (May aid the spread of fire, contribute fuel to the fire, or emit smoke and noxious gases when burning.)
> - Age (Different building codes might be in force at the time of construction, and deterioration of heating, electrical, and other systems might occur over time.)
>
> **Occupancy** (Office, service industry, and manufacturing.)
> - Combustibility (Ability of building's contents to ignite and burn.)
> - Susceptibility (Extent to which fire and its effects will cause damage to materials typical of the occupancy.)
> - Hazards unusual for the occupancy (For example, a cooking facility in a building classified for manufacturing.)
>
> **Protection**
> - Elements of fire protection (Protection, detection, and suppression.)
> - Public fire protection systems (Water supply, fire department, and fire alarm.)
> - Security systems (Protect against theft and vandalism.)
>
> **External Exposure** (Susceptibility to external causes of loss, such as fire from a neighboring building.)
> - Location (Distance from police and fire protection.)
> - Condition of neighboring properties (Abandoned buildings are subject to theft and fire.)
> - Neighborhood characteristics (Vandalism and crime hazards.)

Inland Marine Insurance

Inland marine insurance covers miscellaneous types of property, such as movable property, goods in domestic transit, and property used in transportation and communication. Inland marine insurance is class rated and judgment rated. Insurers use class rating with very common types of insurance, such as a jewelry floater covering an engagement ring and a wedding ring set. Insurers use judgment rating with other inland marine policies covering unique, one-of-a-kind exposures. For example, chances are there is no class rate for a float in a specific parade, so an insurer who is asked to insure such an item of mobile property would have to charge a premium based on personal experience and judgment of the float's loss potential. The insurer might examine rates for physical damage insurance on a semi-trailer and consider the rates typically used to insure a single one-day-long shipment of perishable cargo before arriving at a premium for this unusual exposure.

Because inland marine insurance covers many different miscellaneous types of property, much of which is involved in transportation and communication, the rating basis that can be used for these types of coverages varies widely.

> **Inland Marine Insurance Rating Basis**
>
> These are some examples of a rating basis that can be used in inland marine insurance:
> - Value of property
> - Type of property (jewelry, equipment, property in transit, etc.)
> - Loss history
> - Geographic scope
> - Security measures/protective safeguards
> - Storage location

Commercial General Liability Insurance

Commercial general liability insurance covers liability loss exposures arising from a business organization's premises and operations, its products, or its completed work. Commercial general liability insurance is class rated. Each classification describes a particular type of business operation. Insureds in the same line of business are grouped together because they have similar potentials for loss. Each classification has an applicable rate for each liability coverage.

Many businesses' activities fall into more than one category. Generally, the single category that best describes the business determines the rate for all liability coverage. Only when the insured conducts separate and distinct businesses would more than one classification apply. The major exception is the construction business, in which the variation in hazards requires each construction operation to be separately classified, using judgment rating.

> **Commercial General Liability Insurance Rating Basis**
>
> These are some examples of a rating basis that can be used in commercial general liability insurance:
>
> - Payroll—Rates apply per $1,000 of payroll.
> - Gross sales—Rates apply per $1,000 of gross sales.
> - Area—Rates apply per 1,000 square feet.
> - Admissions—Rates apply per 1,000 admissions. (For a movie theater, each ticket sold would be one admission.)
> - Total cost—Rates apply per $1,000 of total cost as defined and are generally used as a basis for determining premiums on contracted work.
> - Units—Various exposures are rated on a "unit" basis. One example is the number of living units in an apartment building.

The rating basis selected for businesses in each classification is one that reflects the extent of exposures by businesses in those categories. Within workable limits, the rating basis also possesses other desirable features. That is, it reflects the exposure, is readily measurable, is inflation sensitive, and is reasonably simple to work with.

Area (floor space) was used for many years as the rating basis for most retail stores because the potential for customer injury is closely related to a store's size. However, square-foot area is not inflation sensitive, so rates based on area needed to be revised more often than rates based on gross sales if the rates were to be kept commensurate with the exposure. Whenever possible, insurers try to use an inflation-sensitive rating basis rather than a basis like square-foot area or the number of apartment units.

Business Auto Insurance

Business auto insurance covers the insured for liability arising out of the ownership, maintenance, or use of autos and physical damage to autos owned, leased, or hired, by the named insured. Business auto insurance is class rated, similar to personal auto insurance.

The rating basis used in business auto insurance differs somewhat from that used in personal auto insurance.

> **Business Auto Insurance Rating Basis**
>
> These are some examples of a rating basis that can be used in business auto insurance:
>
> - Territory
> - Type of vehicle (gross vehicle weight)
> - Age of vehicle fleet
> - Maintenance history
> - Type of business operation
> - Radius of vehicle operation
> - Drivers
>   - Driving records (moving violations)
>   - Accidents
>   - Driver licensing/training

Workers Compensation Insurance

Workers compensation insurance covers an employer's obligation to pay all compensation and other benefits required of the employer by workers compensation law.

Workers compensation insurance is class rated on a payroll basis. Workers compensation insurance has approximately 600 classifications. This classification system groups types of businesses so that the rate for each classification reflects the exposures common to the business described by that classification. For example, insureds will pay a higher rate for employees in hazardous occupations (such as construction work) than for occupations that fall within the clerical classification. Because some employees of a business often do not share the same hazards as those of the business in general (such as the clerical employees of a construction firm), these employees can be rated separately.

The National Council on Compensation Insurance (NCCI) is the rating bureau responsible for developing workers compensation insurance loss cost data in most states. In some states, all insurers are required to use the same workers compensation insurance rates. However, other states permit insurers to develop their own workers compensation insurance rates.

The rating basis used for workers compensation is payroll (remuneration). What is included and excluded from payroll can make a big difference in the amount an employer pays for workers compensation insurance.

> **Workers Compensation Insurance Rating Basis**
>
> Payroll is the rating basis for workers compensation insurance.
>
> These are some examples of payroll inclusions:
>
> - Wages or salaries
> - Commissions
> - Bonuses
> - Extra pay for overtime work
> - Pay for holidays, vacations, or periods of sickness
> - Annuity plans
>
> These are some examples of payroll exclusions:
>
> - Tips and other gratuities
> - Payments by an employer to group insurance or pension plans
> - Special rewards for invention or discovery
> - Dismissal or severance pay
> - Payments for active military service
> - Employee discounts on goods purchased from the employer

TYPES OF RATING PLANS

Insurers use several types of rating plans to determine premiums.

Insurance rating plans provide insurers with an objective means for determining insurance premiums. An insurance rating system is used to develop rates. Insurers use three types of rates: class rates, individual rates, and judgment rates. Within each of these types of rates are different types of rating plans. Rating plans give a set of directions that specify the criteria used to determine premiums for a particular kind of insurance. Insurers use four types of rating plans: experience rating plans, retrospective rating plans, schedule rating plans, and individual risk premium modification plans.

Experience Rating Plans

Experience rating plans adjust the class rate to be charged for the next policy period to reflect the insured's own loss experience for a period in the recent past. The credit or debit calculated under the plan is applied to the applicable class rate. To be eligible, an insured typically must have at least three years' worth of loss experience and must meet an insurer's minimum account size requirement. If an insured is eligible, an experience rating plan must be used.

Experience rating plan
Rating plan that increases or reduces the premium for a future period based on the insured's own loss experience for a period in the recent past.

In an experience rating plan, for example, an insurer may determine an insured's rates for 20X9 on the basis of that insured's loss experience for years 20X5, 20X6, and 20X7. The insurer would reduce the class rates if the insured's losses were less than average for the classification and increase them if the insured's losses were higher. Because past losses directly affect current and future premiums, experience rating plans provide insureds a direct financial incentive to implement loss control measures.

Workers compensation insurance uses experience rating plans because most employers meet minimum size requirements. For workers compensation, the minimum size requirement is based on the number of employees and is usually set by the state.

> **Four Types of Rating Plans**
> - Experience rating plans—Adjust the class rate to be charged for the next policy period to reflect the insured's loss experience for a period in the recent past
> - Retrospective rating plans—Use the current policy year as the experience period to develop the current year premium
> - Schedule rating plans—In liability insurance, allow underwriters to modify the final premium to reflect factors that the class rate does not include
> - Individual risk premium modification plans—In property insurance, allow underwriters to modify the final premium to reflect factors that the class rate does not include

Retrospective Rating Plans

Retrospective rating plan
Rating plan that increases or reduces an insured's premium for a policy period based on the insured's own losses during the same period.

Retrospective rating plans use the current policy year as the experience period to develop the current year's premium. Under this plan, the insurer charges the insured a deposit premium at the beginning of the policy period. After the end of the policy period, the insurer determines the actual loss experience for that period and charges the insured a final premium for that policy. The insurer adjusts the insured's premium after the end of the policy period to cover losses and loss adjustment expenses incurred by the insured during the policy period, subject to specified minimum and maximum premiums.

The important difference between experience rating and retrospective rating is that experience rating uses loss experience from prior policy periods in determining the premium for the current policy period. Retrospective rating uses the loss experience from the current policy period to determine the premium for the current policy period.

Retrospective rating plans are typically used by organizations large enough to be paying substantial insurance premiums for coverage of their low-to-medium-severity losses. Retrospective rating plans allow such organization to pay lower premiums by partially self-insuring these losses. If the organization experiences low losses, it pays the minimum deposit premium and saves the money it would have spent on more comprehensive insurance. However, if the organization experiences higher-than-expected losses, it pays directly for those higher losses (up to the specified maximum). These organizations usually insure their high-severity losses separately.

Retrospective rating plans are most commonly used in rating workers compensation, auto liability, and general liability insurance policies. Retrospective rating plans can also be used to rate auto physical damage, crime, and glass insurance policies. A single retrospective rating plan can be used for more than one type of loss exposure.

Schedule Rating Plans

Schedule rating plans in liability insurance allow insurers to modify the final premium to reflect factors that the class rate does not include. When underwriting general liability coverage, insurers can apply a schedule rating table to modify class rates, for example, up to a maximum modification of 25 percent.

Schedule rating plan
A rating plan that awards debits and credits based on specific categories, such as the care and condition of the premises or the training and selection of employees.

Schedule Rating Table

The class rates for a risk may be modified in accordance with the following factors as credits or debits according to a schedule, subject to a maximum modification of 25 percent, for example, to reflect these characteristics of the risk that are not reflected in its experience:

- Location
- Premises—condition, care
- Equipment—type, condition, care
- Employees—selection, training, supervision, experience
- Cooperation
  - Medical facilities
  - Safety program

The characteristics listed in a schedule rating table are attributes that are not considered in the development of the class rate but that could affect expected losses. Schedule rating plans for other kinds of insurance are similar to the general liability schedule rating table.

Schedule rating plans are used in commercial auto liability, commercial auto physical damage, general liability, glass, and burglary insurance. Generally, those insureds that are eligible to use experience rating are also eligible for schedule rating. To become eligible for schedule rating, insureds must meet specified minimum premium amounts. As with experience rating, schedule rating must be used on every insured that qualifies. Not every insured will warrant a debit or credit. Some insureds will receive a zero percent modification factor.

Individual Risk Premium Modification Plans

Individual risk premium modification (IRPM) plans are rating plans that achieve the same result as schedule rating plans in that they modify final premiums to reflect factors that the class rate does not include, but they are used in property insurance. The plans are very similar, and insurers often refer to both of them as "schedule rating."

An IRPM plan allows insurers to apply the same debits and credits to property rates that are used in schedule rating plans. Most states limit the amount of the credits or debits that an insurer can apply to an individual insured.

The insurer's judgment is of utmost importance when applying IRPM plans. Application of the debit or credit is based on the insurer's experience in the kind of insurance, the insured's loss experience, the insurer's underwriting policy, and any other relevant factors. Depending on the coverage and type of insured, the insurer should emphasize the physical conditions and hazards of the premises and operations or management's attitude toward loss control.

IRPM plans are used in commercial property to allow the insurer to make adjustments to the final premium using factors that are not reflected in any class rates. Many commercial properties present unique loss exposures to an insurer. The use of IRPM plans provides flexibility to the insurer to tailor the premium to the actual risk presented by the property.

> **Individual risk premium modification (IRPM)**
> A property insurance rating plan that allows underwriters to modify the final premium to reflect factors that the class rate does not include.

SUMMARY

An insurance premium is a periodic payment by the insured to the insurer in exchange for insurance coverage. An insurance premium is calculated by multiplying the rate times the number of exposure units. Insurance rates are developed through insurance rating systems that rely on statistical analysis of past losses to determine what rates insurers should charge. Ideally, an exposure unit should reflect the exposure, be readily measurable, be inflation sensitive, and be reasonably simple. Other factors that are considered in premium determination are the types of marketing systems used, underwriting standards, insurance company ownership, services, coverage, investment income, and cash flow.

Insurers and independent insurance advisory organizations develop insurance rates through insurance rating systems. Insurance advisory organizations gather historical loss costs from insurers to develop prospective loss costs for use by insurers. Insurers use class, individual, or judgment types of rates for insureds in determining insurance premiums for various kinds of insurance.

Some kinds of insurance are class rated by grouping insureds with similar characteristics into the same rating class to capture potential loss frequency and severity of the group. When an insured cannot be readily assigned to the same class, the insured loss exposure is rated individually. For example, a unique factory building can be rated by using a point system to evaluate the risk exposures to determine the applicable insurance rate. Insurers add their allowance for their expenses, profits, and contingencies to arrive at the final rate that they charge insureds for a particular loss exposure.

Personal auto insurance, homeowners insurance, business auto insurance, and workers compensation insurance use class rates because insureds covered by these kinds of insurance can be grouped in the same rating category or rating class, having similar characteristics. For example, in personal auto insurance, insureds may be grouped by type of auto. Commercial property insurance uses class rates or individual rates, depending on the characteristics of the building and contents to be insured. Inland marine insurance uses class rates for common items such as jewelry and judgment rates for unique loss exposures. Commercial general liability insurance generally uses class rates except for cases involving varied hazards in the construction business that therefore require judgment rates.

Insurers also use a rating basis within each kind of insurance to determine premiums. The rating basis is a set of relevant characteristics used to define classes in rating or as factors in individual rating. The rating basis varies among different kinds of insurance and reflects characteristics related to the insured and to the specific kind of insurance coverage.

Insurance rating plans help insurers to determine premiums. Experience rating plans and retrospective rating plans adjust the insured's premium to reflect the insured's actual loss experience. Unlike experience rating, which often uses three years' worth of previous loss experience to modify the premium for the current policy period, retrospective rating plans adjust current-year premiums to reflect current-year loss experience. Schedule rating plans and individual risk premium modification plans allow insurers to adjust rates using insureds' characteristics that usually are not directly recognized in the class rate.

Index

Page numbers in boldface refer to definitions of Key Words and Phrases.

A

Actual cash value, **5.14**
Admitted insurers, **3.7**, 3.17
Adverse selection, **3.11**
Agency bill, **2.6**
Agency expiration list, **3.8**
Agents, **5.16**
Alien insurer, **3.7**
"All-risks" policy, **7.15**
Alternative distribution channels, 3.9
Attorney-in-fact, **3.4**
Automobile liability loss exposure, 9.5–9.6

B

Balance sheet, **5.17**
Basic Form, **7.13**
Basic form coverage, 8.10–8.11
Bodily injury, **5.8**
Book of business, **3.11**
Broad Form, **7.13**
Broad form coverage, 8.11
Building and Personal Property Coverage Form (BPP), **8.8**
Business Auto Coverage Form, **9.8**
Business auto insurance, 9.8, 10.17
Business income insurance, **8.13**
Businessowners policy (BOP), **1.9**

C

Capacity, **4.3**
Captive insurer, **3.5**
Cause of loss, **7.3**
Claim, 3.13
Claimant, **5.4**
Claim file, **5.7**
Claim function, goals of, 5.3–5.4
Claim handling, 2.7, **5.5**
Claim handling process, 5.5–5.9
Claim managers, 5.10
Claim representative, **5.4**, 5.12
Claim supervisors, 5.11
Class rated, **10.3**, 10.9
Collision, **1.8**
Collision coverage, 7.12
Combined ratio, **4.10**
Commercial general liability (CGL), **1.9**
    insurance, 10.16
Commercial insurance, **1.9**
Commercial insurance policies, 1.9–1.10
Commercial liability insurance coverages, 9.7–9.10
Commercial liability loss exposures, 9.3–9.6
Commercial package policy (CPP), **1.9**
Commercial property insurance, 8.7–8.13, 10.14
    covered causes of loss, 8.10–8.13
    covered locations, 8.9–8.10
    covered property, 8.8–8.9
Commercial property loss exposures, 8.3–8.7
Completed operations liability exposure, **9.5**
Condition, **6.11**
Constructive total loss, **5.14**
Contents, **8.4**
Coverage A—Bodily Injury and Property Damage Liability, 9.7
Coverage B—Personal and Advertising Injury Liability, 9.8
Coverage C—Medical Payments, 9.8
Crash manual, **5.13**
Crime insurance, **1.9**
Customer service, 2.7, 4.12
Customer service representatives, 5.14

D

Damages, **5.12**
Declarations, **6.4**
DICE method, 6.14
Direct bill, **2.6**
Direct response distribution channel, **3.9**
Direct writer marketing system, **2.9**, 3.9
Domestic insurer, **3.7**
Draft authority, **5.16**
Dwelling insurance, 7.12

E

Earned premiums, **4.9**
Endorsement, **6.6**
Excess and surplus lines (E&S) insurance, **3.7**
Exclusion, **6.12**
Exclusive agency marketing system, **2.9**, 3.8
Exclusive agent, **3.8**

Expense ratio, **4.9**
Experience rating plan, **10.19**
Expert systems, **4.4**
Exposure unit, **1.5**, 10.4
Extra expenses, **8.13**

F

Fair rental value, **7.6**
False arrest, **9.8**
Field claim representative, **5.12**
File-and-use law, **3.18**
Final rate, **10.10**
First-party claim, **5.3**
Flex rating law, **3.18**
Flood insurance, 7.16
Foreign insurer, **3.7**

G

General liability insurance, 9.7
  Coverage A—Bodily Injury and Property Damage Liability, 9.7
  Coverage B—Personal and Advertising Injury Liability, 9.8
  Coverage C—Medical Payments, 9.8
Government insurers, 3.5
Guaranty fund, **3.21**

H

Hazard, **3.12**
Homeowners insurance, 10.13
Homeowners insurance policy, 7.4–7.7
  Section I – Property Coverages, 7.5–7.6
  Section II – Liability Coverages, 7.6–7.7

I

Incurred losses, **5.17**
Independent agency and brokerage marketing system, **2.8**, 3.8
Individual rate, **10.10**
Individual risk premium modification (IRPM), **10.22**
Inherent vice, **8.12**
Inland marine insurance, **7.15**, 10.16
Inside claim representative, **5.12**
Insurable interest, **6.14**
Insurance advisory organization, **10.6**
Insurance broker, **3.8**
Insurance marketing systems, 2.8
Insurance policy, **1.4**, 3.18
  types of, 1.7–1.10
Insurance rates, 3.18, 10.3
Insurance regulation, 3.14–3.21
Insurance Regulatory Information System (IRIS), **3.20**

Insurance Services Office (ISO), **7.5**
Insured, 2.3, **5.10**
Insurer, **1.3**, 2.3
  functions, 3.10–3.14
  solvency, 3.20
Insuring agreement, **6.11**

J

Judgment rating, **10.10**

L

Latent defect, **8.12**
Law of large numbers, **1.5**–1.7
Legal liability, **1.8**
  basis for, 9.3
Liability loss exposure, **7.4**
Libel, **9.8**
Licensed insurer, **3.7**
Licensing, 3.16
Lloyds association, 3.4
Loss adjustment expenses (LAE), **5.17**
Loss control, 3.13
Loss costs, **10.9**
Loss exposure, **1.3**
Loss ratio, **4.9**
Loss reserves, 5.7, 5.17
Lost income, 8.6

M

Mandatory rate law, **3.18**
Manuscript policy, **6.4**
Market conduct regulation, **3.19**
Marketing system, **3.8**
Miscellaneous provisions, 6.13
Modular policy, **6.3**
Moral hazard, **6.12**
Morale, or attitudinal, hazard, **6.12**
Mutual insurer, **3.4**

N

National Association of Insurance Commissioners (NAIC), **3.20**
Negligence, **9.3**
Nonadmitted insurers, **3.17**

O

Open competition, **3.18**
Operations liability exposure, **9.4**
Other than collision coverage, 7.11
Outside claim representative, **5.12**

P

Package policy, **7.4**
Peril, **1.8**
Personal and advertising injury, **9.8**
Personal auto insurance policy, 7.7–7.12
    liability coverage, 7.8–7.9
    medical payments coverage, 7.9–7.10
    physical damage coverage, 7.11–7.12
    uninsured motorists coverage, 7.10–7.11
Personal injury, **5.8**
Personal inland marine insurance, 7.15
Personal insurance, **2.3**
Personal insurance policies, 1.8
Personal liability coverage, **1.8**
Personal property, **7.3**, 8.4
Personal property and liability loss exposures, 7.3–7.4
Personal property of others, 8.9
Personal umbrella insurance, 7.13
Physical damage coverage, 7.11
Policy provision, **6.8**
Policyholders' surplus, **3.17**
Pooling, **1.4**
Predictive modeling, **4.5**
Premises liability exposure, **9.4**
Premises and operations liability loss exposure, 9.4
Premium, **1.3**, 10.3
    allocation, 1.14–1.15
    audit, **3.14**
    calculation, 10.4
    collection, 2.6
Pricing coverage, 3.11, 4.11
Primary insurer, **3.5**
Prior approval law , **3.18**
Producer, **2.4**–2.5
    functions, 2.5
Product mix, 4.11
Products and completed operations liability loss exposure, 9.4–9.5
Products liability exposure, **9.5**
Property damage, **5.8**
Property loss exposure, **7.3**
Prospecting, 2.5
Prospective loss costs, **10.9**

Q

Question-and-answer method, 6.14

R

Rate, **10.3**
Real property, **7.3**, 8.4
Reciprocal insurance exchange, **3.4**
Reinsurance, **3.5**
Reinsurer, **3.5**
Reserves, **3.20**

Residual market, **3.6**
Retention ratio, **4.11**
Retrospective rating plan, **10.20**
Risk, **1.3**
Risk management review, 2.6

S

Sales, 2.6
Salvage, **5.14**
Schedule rating plan, **10.21**
Scheduled coverage, **6.9**
Self-contained policy, **6.3**
Self-insured retention, **7.15**
Single limit basis, **7.9**
Slander, **9.8**
Solvency, **3.15**
Solvency surveillance, **3.20**
Special Form, **7.13**
Special form (open perils) coverage, 8.11
Specialized claim representatives, 5.12
Split limits basis, **7.9**
Standard form, **3.12**
Statute, **9.3**
Stock insurer, **3.3**
Subrogation, **5.8**
Subscriber, **3.4**
Success ratio, **4.11**–4.12
Surplus lines laws, **3.17**

T

Technical specialists, 5.13
Telephone claim representative, **5.12**
Third-party administrator, **5.13**
Third-party claim, **5.3**
Tort, **9.3**
Total loss, **5.14**
Transfer, 1.3–1.4

U

Umbrella liability insurance, 9.10
Umbrella liability policy, **1.10**
Umbrella policy, **7.13**
Underwriter, **4.4**
Underwriting, **3.11**, 4.3-4.13
    expenses, **5.17**
    loss, **4.10**
    profit, **4.10**
    process 4.4
    purpose of, 4.3–4.4
    results, measurement of, 4.9–4.12
Unfair trade practices acts, **3.19**
Uninsured motorists coverage, 7.10
Unlicensed insurer, **3.7**
Use-and-file law, **3.18**

W

Workers compensation and employers liability insurance, **9.9**
Workers compensation insurance, **1.9**, 10.18
Workers compensation statute, **9.9**
Written premium, **4.4**